The Crimes in Times Journal

Volume II

Victorian Rules

First Edition

Written by

Dr. Hollis A. Palmer

Deep Roots Publications
Saratoga Springs, N. Y.

The Crimes in Time Journal
Vol. II

Victorian Rules

Published by:

Deep Roots Publications
P. O. Box 114
Saratoga Springs, NY 12866

Library of Congress Number 00191948

ISBN 0-9671713-1-8

Palmer, Hollis Albert.
    The crimes in times journal. Vol. II / Hollis A.
    Palmer.—1st ed.
    p. cm.
    LCCN 00-191948
    ISBN 0-9671713-8-1

    1. Crime-New York (State)-History-19th century.
    I. Title

This book is dedicated to my students for the past two years

AJ
Amy
Dan
Eric
Jacob
Paul
Syd
Yatir

You challenged me every day and in every way.
May you question your future teachers as inquired of me.

Special thanks to

Nicole Stein

Again she gives my thoughts direction

And especially

Jim Russo

For letting us figure out how to add pictures.

Table of Contents

A Legacy Lost

On Monday evening, October 29th, the headlines in the *Batavia Daily News* told of a wealthy local farmer who had been returned to Batavia in the custody of the sheriff. He had been arrested in New York City on a charge of bigamy. For some time the farmer's wife had noted that when he went on errands he was frequently driving all the way into LeRoy rather than the two miles into Batavia. The previous week, when he returned from one of his excursions to LeRoy, his wife went through the pockets of his jacket. In one of the pockets was a letter from New York City addressed to Charles Porter (Porter was the husband's middle name not the family's name). "Her womanly curiosity was excited..." so she read the enclosed letter which was addressed, "My Darling Husband." The signature followed the closing, "Your Loving Wife." When the husband left for New York City the next day the wife immediately consulted a lawyer. The lawyer and the farmer's wife went together to a judge and had a warrant issued for the arrest of the husband on a charge of bigamy. The next morning the forty-year-old husband was arrested in the Continental Hotel in Manhattan in the company of a woman half his age.

These headlines, as intriguing as they were to those who enjoy life through the misery of others, were nothing like those that would follow two short days later.

Murder

The plan had been set for days. Unfortunately for everyone involved, the over anxious couple had forced the husband to rush the timing. Edward Newton "Newt" Rowell was hiding in his well-appointed home hours before the time his friends had agreed to be there. As he waited silently in the unlit front parlor of his handsome new house, he could hear the sounds of two women in the back of the house making tea and dinner in the kitchen.

Rowell had ample reasons to believe his wife was being unfaithful. To confirm his trepidations he planned to catch his wife and her lover together. Rowell, a salesman, invented a story about leaving town on a business trip. Actually he had stayed for two days in a local hotel. In the evening of the second day that he was supposedly away his worst fears were realized when, at 7:30, there was a knock on the front door of his house. Although his wife had expected her guest an hour earlier, the visitor had had trouble finding the new house. The motives for his outing made it impossible for the caller to ask for directions, so he had to walk the streets of Batavia until he found the house.

Rowell, who was secreted away in the front salon, heard his wife answer the door. He listened to her address a man known to both of them from their former home in Utica. Mrs. Jennie Rowell greeted her guest, "I am almost sorry you came." Both her husband and her visitor noted she said she was *almost* sorry not that she was sorry. She went on to say, "Your telegram was taken to the box factory and I am afraid Palmer saw it." Until the previous month, William Palmer and her husband had been in business together. At that time her husband had asked Palmer to buy out his share of the business. The relationship between the two men was not severed as her husband had stayed on as an employee in Palmer's box factory. The wife knew that Palmer was suspicious of her behavior. If he read the note, and he almost inevitably would have, he would have known of her planned dalliance.

Jennie could tell that her words were not deterring her guest from wanting to come inside. She added yet another reason for him not to enter, "I am afraid he will be watching us." No one could tell from the words whether the "he" was her husband or his former business partner, William Palmer.

To those mired in the Victorian virtues of

A DISHONORED HUSBAND'S SWIFT VENGEANCE

MR. E. N. ROWELL, A MERCHANT OF BATAVIA, N. Y., DISCOVERING JOHNSON L. LYNCH, A UTICA LAWYER, IN FLAGRANTE DELICTO WITH HIS WIFE, MEETS OUT SPEEDY JUSTICE TO THE DESTROYER OF HIS HOME.

ARTIST ILLUSTRATION OF SHOOTING OF JOHNSON LYNCH BY BUSINESSMAN E. N. ROWELL.
THIS GRAPHIC APPEARED IN *THE NATIONAL POLICE GAZETTE.*
TO MAKE THE STORY MORE INTRIGUING THE ARTIST TOOK LIBERTIES SUCH AS THE SHOULDERLESS DRESS WORN BY MRS. JENNIE ROWELL.

1883, gentlemanly tradition held that the visitor was expected to leave at the least protest of his married paramour. To enter now was an invasion, not an invitation. Johnson Lynch, a lawyer from Utica and a man born into the most prestigious of families, was not to be deterred. After a four-hour train ride, Lynch pushed for his reward saying, "Oh he won't bother his head about us."

Jennie Rowell held the door to prevent her guest admission to her house. She protested that regardless of Lynch's words of confidence she was still afraid. She even added that her husband knew of her infidelities saying, "I have promised my husband faithfully that I would have nothing to do with you."

Lynch, the exasperated lover, responded, "Then why in the world didn't you write me so; instead of writing me to come?" Mrs. Rowell apparently felt the company at the door was worth the risk, as she ended her protest and invited him in for dinner.

There were four places set at the dining room table. They were for Jennie Rowell, Johnson Lynch, a woman neighbor who had helped prepare the meal and the neighbor's husband when he arrived. Uncertain as to when the neighbor's husband would arrive, and rather than let the dinner get cold, the three in the house sat down to din-

2

ner. While they ate the opening course in the dining room, Rowell slipped silently out of the front salon and up the stairs to the second floor, where he hid in one of his children's bedrooms.

It was only moments after the three sat down when the doorbell rang for a second time. Expecting her husband, the neighbor answered the door. As anticipated it was the woman helper's husband calling for her. She invited her husband to join the group for dinner, telling him, "We are just setting down to supper." He begged off, insisting that he had business that evening and he and his wife would have to leave. Jennie came out of the dining room and joined in extending an invitation to the husband for dinner and games of cards after the meal. She implied that there was someone else in the house that was going to leave at 10:30. Jennie was not able to convince her friend's husband to stay.

Alone, Jennie Rowell and Johnson Lynch resumed partaking of the rest of the meal she had prepared. As they conversed over the simple repast, Newt Rowell listened at the top of the stairs. What pain he felt as he heard the conversation of the lovers was never reported but it was questioned why he did not confront the two of them while they were alone in the dining room. Even more disconcerting to those who would later read about the case was his choice not to confront the two after they left the table to sit on the couch in the dark parlor where he had hidden earlier that evening. Having a reasonable understanding of what was transpiring in the room below, Rowell did not confront the two while they embraced in the parlor.

Eventually the couple opted to leave the settee in the parlor, choosing to adjourn to the comfort of a bed upstairs. Hearing their move-

BIRDSEYE ILLUSTRATION OF BATAVIA STATION DRAWN A FEW YEARS BEFORE THE SHOOTING
NOTE THE NATIONAL HOTEL WAS BUILT APPROXIMATELY WHERE THE X HAS BEEN PLACED
COURTESY HOLLAND PATTON MUSEUM

ments Rowell moved silently back from the open stair railing into one of his daughter's bedrooms. Rowell listened intently as his wife and Lynch moved into the master bedroom, his bedroom. He overheard the sounds emanating from the dark room as the two lovers began to embrace more intimately on the bed.

As the couple began to remove Lynch's clothes, Rowell entered the room. He pulled a small quantity of ground pepper from his jacket pocket intent on rubbing it in Lynch's eyes. Lynch was large and the room was very dark. In the extreme darkness of the bedroom, Rowell totally missed his target. The pepper slipped from Rowell's hand and spilled onto the bed. Having

tipped off Lynch to his presence, Rowell pulled a revolver from his pocket and fired a shot at the dark shadows on the bed. He missed both people as the bullet passed between the lovers before being trapped in a pillow. The bullet was fired so close to the two lovers that burnt powder marks were found on each of their cheeks. The bullet actually severed some of Jennie's hair as it passed by her head. As Lynch started to rise from the bed, Rowell backed slowly toward the door, firing a second round. This bullet also missed its intended target and wedged in the plaster over the fireplace. Trapped in a strange room Lynch switched from a defensive posture to an aggressive one. Lynch came off of the bed and charged at the

THE HOUSE ON BANK STREET, IN BATAVIA, SCENE OF THE SHOOTING.

ROWELL ARRANGED WITH THE BUILDER TO HAVE THE HOUSE FINISHED LESS THAN A WEEK BEFORE THE SHOOTING. THERE ARE THREE HOUSES IN A ROW THAT LOOK THE SAME. ON THE RIGHT IS THE PORCH THAT ROWELL STOOD ON TO CALL TO HIS NEIGHBOR FOR HELP.

doorway. Wisely, Rowell had backed out of the door and to the left, away from the stairway that led to the front door. Lynch seized this opportunity to flee and while holding up his pants he ran for the stairway. When Lynch reached the first step of the beautiful wooden stairway, Rowell fired a third shot. This shot entered Lynch's body near his right shoulder blade, glanced down through a lung, and severed his aorta. From this point down the stairs small splatters of Lynch's blood appeared. Acting on sheer instinct, Lynch did not stop, but continued his quest of the safety that was just beyond the front door. His ire burning, Rowell was in hot pursuit. Only a few steps behind his mark, Rowell dropped the pistol on the stairs and grabbed a slingshot (a rock encased in a sock). He intended to use the third weapon on Lynch's head.

At the bottom of the stairs, Lynch continued to sprint, almost reaching the front door. Just before his hand grasped the door handle, Lynch coughed once, spilling blood onto the door, then he started to fall. At exactly the same time as he began to tumble Rowell swung the slingshot at Lynch's head. The blow struck its mark but did little damage as Lynch was already moving in the same direction as the slingshot. Lynch twisted on his way to the floor, his life nearly over.

In the last moments of his life, Lynch pulled his right arm up onto his chest as if grabbing for his damaged heart. Lynch never moved again. Rapidly a pool of blood formed around his chest and head. During his fall Lynch's legs twisted in an unnatural pose.

There would always be a debate over whether there were actually four shots fired. Four empty casings were found in the gun. The mark where the pin hits the bullet was very different on one of the empty casings than on the other three.

Still dressed Jennie Rowell came running down the stairs, screaming at her husband. Rowell waited only a moment before he went out onto his front porch and called for help.

Hearing the shots and the cry for help twenty-nine-year-old Eugene Swanson, Rowell's next door neighbor, went out onto his own porch and asked "What's the trouble over there?" Swanson had been sitting in his living room, reading the newspaper when he heard Rowell's call for help. Swanson, a tailor in the village, claimed later that he heard four shots – two in rapid succession and two more after some rumbling noises.

"For God's sake come over quick, I have shot a man," Rowell shouted back. Swanson went quickly back into his own home, put on his shoes, coat and hat before departing for the Rowell house. After having gathered his outdoor wear Swanson went back in the street. Perhaps Swanson was fearful of his new neighbor, since he went to the house on the other side to ask a second neighbor, Charles Read, to go with him to Rowell's. Read, a sewing machine agent, lived in the second house north of Rowell's. Together, Read and Swanson went to find out what had happened. Newt Rowell had returned to the foyer of his house when the two neighbors reached his front porch. When he had gone back inside Rowell had left the front door open.

When the two neighbors entered, Rowell was kneeling near the prostrate man – a pitcher of water was sitting on the floor. He called to his neighbors, "Come on in here and help." It was obvious to the men that Rowell had been using the water in an ineffective attempt to bring the man back to consciousness. Rowell went on, "I found this man in my house and shot him." Both neighbors were struck by how calm Rowell was despite the circumstances.

Read asked, "Is he a burglar?"

"No, I found him seducing my wife and shot him," was Rowell's unruffled reply. He went on to ask his neighbors, "What shall we do?"

There is always a leader and in this situation Read took charge. Reasonably sure that the man on the floor was already dead, Read suggested to Rowell that they should send for the coroner. Read dispatched Swanson for the coroner and to get a police officer. Before Swanson left the house both he and Read were struck by Jennie Rowell's behavior. She just kept walking up and down the stairs. Eventually, she stopped and called out, "Mr. Rowell how could you do such a

JOHNSON LYNCH GREAT-GRANDSON
OF PRESIDENT JOHN ADAMS

AT FIVE FEET TEN INCHES TALL AND ONE HUNDRED EIGHTY POUNDS
LYNCH WAS DESCRIBED AS BEING HERCULEAN IN BUILD. HE WAS ALSO AN
EXCELLENT DANCER AND HAD A MELODIOUS VOICE.
PICTURE FROM *THE NATIONAL POLICE GAZETTE*.

BUSINESSMAN E. NEWTON (NEWT) ROWELL

ROWELL HAD RECENTLY STARTED A PAPER BOX FACTORY IN BATAVIA. HIS COMPANY MANUFACTURED THE
BOXES THAT WERE USED OVER PATENT MEDICINES AND COSMETICS. THIS PICTURE OF ROWELL IS AS A
YOUNGER MAN AND IS PROBABLY BASED ON THE PICTURE THAT WAS ON HIS FRAMED
MARRIAGE LICENSE THAT HUNG ON THE WALL IN THE BEDROOM.
PICTURE FROM *THE NATIONAL POLICE GAZETTE.*

cruel thing? What a fearful disgrace!"

Rowell answered his wife, "Yes, Jennie but it is done."

"Why did you do it?"

"Jennie, I could not help it," Rowell replied, reminding his wife that he had warned her over and over against seeing Lynch.

"What will they do with you now?" Jennie asked more as an intellectual question than ones asked out of passion.

Read was near the body on the floor when Rowell responded, "Well I suppose they will put me in jail." By this time Rowell was climbing the stairs to be closer to his wife.

Jennie ascended even further, staying away from her husband, "You will be hung for this."

Read had come to know Rowell while the house was being built and always considered him to be a devoted family man. Even as caring as Read envisioned Rowell, Read was totally taken aback by how compassionate Rowell was to his wife even in these circumstances. Rowell reached out to hold Jennie saying in a calm voice, " I am the one that shall have to pay for it." The remote Jennie rejected her husband's attempted embrace.

Not being able to console his wife Rowell came back down the stairs. As he passed the pistol on the steps, Rowell casually picked it up. It did not appear to Read that Rowell was trying to be sneaky as he pocketed the gun. Read felt that Rowell's retrieval of the gun was an instinctive act rather than a deliberate one. Read didn't think it wise to leave a hand gun in the possession of a man who had just used it to kill someone so he reached over and removed the gun from Rowell's coat. Rowell offered no resistance to being free of the gun saying, "It is empty, I fired five shots." (It appears that in the heat of the action Rowell had lost count himself.) Read placed the gun in one of his own jacket pockets without looking to see how many times it had been fired.

Rowell returned to the prostrate form on the floor, asking Read, "Do you think he is dead?" Read assure Rowell that he was pretty sure that the man on the floor was deceased.

***

On his way downtown for help, Swanson came upon a young boy out for a late evening walk. Swanson sent him to get a police officer while he went for the coroner. It took Swanson only a couple of minutes to reach Coroner Tozier's office. Tozier, upon hearing the news, left within minutes for Rowell's home. As Tozier and Swanson passed Dr. Morse's office, they went inside and asked him to come to the scene. Tozier then left on foot for Rowell's. Dr. Morse dove his buggy to the Rowell's house, providing Swanson with a ride.

***

The two doctors arrived at the Rowells' almost exactly the same time. Uncertain where his wife was Rowell asked, "Doctor, I wish you to go upstairs or on the stairway and see to my wife." Morse took on the responsibility of Mrs. Rowell, while Tozier stayed with the fallen man. Having watched Dr. Morse go to his wife, Rowell was standing at the foot of the stairs when he asked Dr. Tozier if the man on the floor was dead. Dr. Tozier checked the man's vital signs and said yes he was dead. Upon hearing the news Rowell exhibited one of the few signs of emotion that he imparted all evening. Out of anguish, he struck the banister with both hands.

At about this point in the evening two things happened. Rowell went upstairs to check on his wife and Read handed the pistol to the coroner. As Coroner Tozier examined the pistol, he noted that four of the five chambers had been fired. There was a fifth unspent bullet in the gun. Tozier also noted that there was blood on the stairs commencing at about the third step from the top. He noted that the blood on the stair was only a smattering and the vast majority was on the foyer floor. Over the course of that evening and the following morning, the coroner would locate three of the bullets. Whatever happened to the fourth, if there was a fourth, was never ascertained.

After Swanson returned with the two doctors, Read felt less responsible for maintaining a watch over Rowell and began wandering around the house. At one point he went into the dining room. He noted that there were four place settings. Three of them had been used. More importantly there was "considerable food" that was not disturbed. The implication was simple, those who were present had an appetite that food would not satisfy. The selection on the table made it obvious that the meal, for that period, was to be a celebration. On the table were oysters, cold meat, celery and cakes. There were also unfinished cups of coffee on the table. It was apparent that those who had been at the table felt compelled to undertake other activities more important than cleaning up.

It was only minutes after the doctors got to the Rowell house when two police officers arrived. One glance at Coroner Tozier and the policemen understood the gravity of the situation. Tozier told the two officers that Rowell and his wife were upstairs with Dr. Morse. The officers walked around Lynch's prostrate body on their way to talk to the witnesses.

When the policemen got to the second floor they noted the relationship between the couple. Mrs. Rowell's concerns remained focused on the fallen Lynch – none of her distress was for her husband. Despite her behavior, all those present that night noted how Rowell was affectionate and tender toward Jennie. Amazingly, Rowell exhibited no signs of anger even as his wife's attention centered on her slain lover. Jennie Rowell continuously paced around the bedchamber, her hands nervously wringing a towel.

Throughout the evening, Jennie Rowell's behavior would strike anyone who saw her in a dramatic way. At one point she asked her husband to wash the blood off Lynch's face. No one witnessed Rowell complying with such a strange request.

In front of the officers and physicians Jennie Rowell kept asking her husband how he could have done such a cruel thing. She asked, "Why didn't you just kick him or something?" The answer was obvious to everyone. Rowell was just over five feet in height and weighed about one hundred and ten pounds. Lynch, who was described as Herculean in build, was five feet ten inches tall and weighed in excess of one hundred and eighty pounds. Had Rowell attempted to

kick Lynch he would probably have been the one lying on the floor in a puddle of blood.

Holding her burnt hair as evidence, Jennie accused Rowell of almost shooting her. He responded, "I would never do such a thing."

Although not fearful of the assailant, the two policemen turned to Rowell and said, "We will have to take charge of you."

Jennie Rowell asked, "Where will you take him?"

"To jail, I suppose," one of the deputies responded.

Rowell surrendered quite peacefully, asking his wife for a kiss before he left. She responded, "How can I after you have done such a cruel thing." One of the deputies took Rowell downstairs; the second remained upstairs with Mrs. Rowell and Dr. Morse.

By now a crowd had formed in front of the Rowell house. The deputy in charge of Rowell knew it was getting time to take him down to the village jail. Rather than lead him through the throng out front, the deputy took Rowell out the back door through the garden and down a side street. Rowell was so calm and accepting that the deputy didn't even use restraints on him. Rowell was appreciative of the respect given and began talking openly to the deputy. The following is a summation of what was reportedly told to the deputy in the conversation on the way to the jail.

Rowell said that some of his friends were supposed to come to the house and help catch Lynch in the act. They planned to take Lynch's clothes and throw him out into the street naked. They were then going to mail the highly-political Lynch's clothes back to various newspapers in Utica. It was hoped that the disgrace would serve its purpose. Rowell went on to say that Lynch and Jennie had started their intimacy too early. Rowell told how the two had first left the table for a couch in the parlor. That would have been okay but then they had gone into his bedroom where they began their play before even turning down the bed covers. The sounds the couple began making were too much for the calm Rowell. He had rushed into the room with the intent of putting pepper in Lynch's eyes. Unfortunately, the room was too dark. Rowell could not make out Lynch's features well enough to get the pepper in his eyes. That was when all hell had broken loose.

As the deputy and Rowell were walking downtown they passed William Palmer, Rowell's former business partner and current employer, in the company of a couple of his friends. The four men were walking toward the Rowell house. It was dark and at first Palmer did not recognize Rowell in the company of the police officer. After the two groups passed Palmer realized it was his friend. Palmer went back to the deputy and Rowell and took Rowell's arm asking, "What are you doing here?"

"I am under arrest," Rowell responded.

"What for?"

"I shot that man," Rowell replied.

"Did you hurt him seriously?"

"He is dead," Rowell stated as a simple fact.

Rowell asked his former partner, to go to the hotel and gather his belongings. Palmer, in a state of shock, said he doubted he had the money to pay the bill. Rowell handed him a five-dollar bill to settle the tab. The deputy took Rowell by the arm and gently took him toward the village jail. When they resumed their walk the deputy informed Rowell that perhaps he should stop talking until he consulted his attorney. It was obvious, from the very beginning, that Rowell was respected by those charged with his custody.

Reaching the village jail, the deputy escorted Rowell into what was known as the police court. There, Rowell sat at a table alone awaiting the judge. By the time the police court judge finally entered the room the word of what had happened had spread throughout the village. The inquisitive were attracted to the court like those who today are compelled to look at an accident as they drive by. As Rowell sat in the courtroom awaiting the judge, members of the crowd that had gathered felt he "looked like a dying man." His demeanor was so broken he appeared "about ready to give out, both physically and mentally."

When the judge finally arrived quite a crowd had gathered in the small room. Rowell sat with his head tilted forward. He was totally calm, so much so that when his trial finally came three months later the deputies who were in the room that night would both say his demeanor was unnatural. The only word Rowell spoke to the judge was when he was asked for a plea. Rowell said in a soft voice, "Not guilty."

After the judge ordered Rowell held for further investigation, he was taken to the village jail where one of the deputies searched his clothes before allowing him to enter the cell. In an inner coat pocket the deputy found an oval picture case. There was a dark purple velvet border surrounding the picture of a younger Jennie Rowell. The deputy looked at the frame and said, "You don't want that do you?" Not hearing a response from the prisoner the deputy went on, "You'd better let me keep that."

There are conflicts in the reports of exactly how Rowell responded to his wife's portrait being taken from him. In many newspapers it was reported that he said something to the effect, "For God's sake don't take that." Or, "Let me keep that, for God's sake." At the trial that followed one witness testified that he made neither remark. What is known is that he was allowed to have his wife's picture in the cell the entire time between the shooting and the trial.

***

At the house the crowd continued to gather, as word of the shooting spread. Their curiosity aroused, some members of the crowd were so audacious that they actually entered the Rowell house to see the scene first hand. To prevent the horror from becoming a spectacle someone suggested that the doors be locked. This only screened out those seeking a direct examination. People continued to walk up onto the veranda to look at the grisly scene through the glass in the doors. Exasperated by the gall of the crowd, someone inside decided to pin newspapers over the windows to block the view.

The deputy who remained at the Rowells' house and the coroner wanted suitable shelter away from the scene for Jennie for the night. In search of suitable accommodation, the coroner took Mrs. Rowell to the home of the King family. The Kings were one of Jennie's few friends in Batavia. King, a successful local brewer, was not amused when he opened the door where he was greeted by a deputy sheriff. Explaining the situation, the deputy asked Mr. King to provide shelter for Mrs. Rowell for the night. At first King refused to let Jennie stay. It took a while but eventually King was convinced by his wife and the deputy that despite her lack of virtue Mrs. Rowell was not a danger. More importantly, King was assured his family would not be scorned by accepting a fallen woman into their home for one night.

Dr. Morse would later agree to be interviewed by *The Buffalo Express*. In the interview he points out that while he was with Jennie that evening she admitted to him her guilt in inviting Lynch to her home. She even quoted Shakespeare during their discussion. She used a variety of quotes that the doctors said implied "when a man loses what he does not miss there is nothing out of the way about it." The doctor remarked that her words would "put many a good actress to blush." The doctor's quotes about her choice of clothes did much to add to the flames feeding off Jennie's reputation. "She was dressed in elegant silks and satins that evening. With diamond earrings and finger rings of the same. She had once been a fine looking woman, but now shows signs of debauchery."

***

The Rowells' problems began the preceding August, if not before. In all probability the problems began when they lived in Utica.

In February 1880, William Palmer and Edward Newton Rowell decided it was time that they moved their paper box business from Utica to Batavia. The two men had grown up together in Utica and had been friends for more than thirty years. Since Rowell was only thirty-six years old at the time of the shooting, it can be safely said that the two were lifelong friends. They had chosen as an enterprise the manufacture of paper boxes. The boxes they made were the type commonly used to package a druggist's prescription medicines. In making the move to Batavia the two had also chosen to leave their homes and extended families in Utica. In the early 1880s Batavia was a boomtown. In the two years they had been in Batavia the population had grown almost exactly fifty percent from five thousand to seventy-five hundred.

The exact date that the tribulations in the Rowell family began to take shape is unclear. William Palmer had been convinced for some time that Jennie Rowell was untrue to her husband. In early August, Jennie Rowell, in what was described as a fit of anger, went into the box factory and told Palmer, "It would be a little more agreeable to me to be allowed to read my own letters first." The implication was clear. She felt that he was somehow getting into the family's post office box, stealing or, at the very least, reading her correspondences. Palmer's ego may have been able to stand the implication but Jennie had made the classic mistake of making the comment in front of the employees of the factory. Effectively embarrassed, Palmer's actions over the course of the next three months imply he was on a quest for revenge.

On the twentieth of August, while they were at the box factory, Palmer asked Rowell if his wife had said anything to him about his opening any of her correspondences. Rowell said that indeed she had shown him the backside of an envelope, saying that Palmer had opened it before she received the letter. Palmer asked if she had also shown him the letter the envelope contained. Rowell said that she had not. Rowell was disturbed by his partner's actions. Palmer told his partner that the letter would have told far more than the open envelope. For Palmer, Jennie's telling her husband of the perceived invasion of her privacy was the last straw. Palmer went on to tell his partner of his suspicions regarding Jennie's relationships. Palmer's motives in telling Rowell of his wife's behavior were not necessarily virtuous, as it would come out later that he had probably tried to gain Jennie's affections for himself.

Palmer maintained that on at least two occasions Jennie Rowell had implied that she sought company outside her marriage. The first time she had remarked that her husband was "as cold as an iceberg." According to Palmer, when he asked her what this meant, Jennie stated that her husband's lack of affection allowed her the privilege of seeking the attention of others. Palmer maintained that on that occasion he had told her that her husband's behavior could not be used as a justification, but only as an excuse.

Palmer reported the second conversation happened while they still lived in Utica. In that occurrence, Jennie said she had a fondness for tall men. Jennie was almost exactly five feet tall. When she was younger she was beautiful but, though only in her late twenties, she had gained weight and her hair was showing some white. Her face still reflected the beauty that had, at one time, made her one of the belles of her small community of Clayville. Continuing with her story about tall men Jennie supposedly told Palmer that she had had one recently. When Palmer inquired how Jennie was getting away with having a gentleman friend she had told him that she wasn't worried about her husband finding out, since he was slow and many things would escape him.

Reflecting back on a conversation in Utica, Palmer could remember Jennie saying that she was going to have a tall boy with a straight nose and no one at ninety-three would be the father. The ninety-three was a reference to 93 Howard Avenue, the Rowell residence while they lived in Utica. This home, which is now gone, stood on the northeast corner of Leah and Howard Streets. The other family in the house was that of George Williams. Mrs. Williams was believed to be the lady who led Jennie into a life of deceit.

It should be noted that the conversation that Palmer referenced would have been very uncommon in Victorian society. Men and women, who were not related, would not have engaged in conversations that implied infidelity, unless they were testing each other's intentions.

Palmer would cite one other occasion where he had some basis for his beliefs that Jennie was seeking outside company. While he and Rowell were in business in Utica he had sent a boy over to do errands for Mrs. Rowell. The boy told him later that Jennie had asked him to deliver a note to a law office over a store in downtown Utica. The office was the one used by Johnson Lynch and his uncle Arthur B. Johnson (Lynch's mother's brother). A. B. Johnson, the elder partner, was the politician behind the scenes in Republican politics in New York State. Palmer had filed away these bits of information like parts of a puzzle. Resting in the recesses of his mind, the stories of Jennie with other men were getting ripe so they could be used later.

Rowell and Palmer had divided their responsibilities in the manufacturing operation. Rowell was responsible for sales and Palmer, production. This arrangement caused Rowell to be out of town for up to four weeks, three times a year. Palmer told Rowell that, during his trip in early August, Jennie was seen walking from the train station late one evening. Palmer was tipped off to the behavior by a message from Jennie, asking for a girl to be sent down from the box factory to take care of the house as she was "going on a visit." Palmer's suspicions, aroused by Jennie's request, caused him to begin his own investigation. Based on the time of her arrival he learned that Jennie had gone to Rochester. Palmer went to Rochester where he checked the hotel registries for the night in question. Palmer was able to establish that Jennie had met Lynch. Angered by Jennie's behavior toward him, Palmer provided Rowell with the exact date and the name of the hotel where Lynch and Jennie had met. Palmer invited Lynch to go to the hotel and check the registry for himself. Palmer also told Rowell that there were other names on the register that night that he might also find intriguing.

A few days later Rowell went to Rochester. At one of the finer hotels he noted that his wife had registered under the name of Jennie Potter, while the same night Lynch had stayed there and used his own name. Upon determining for himself that his wife had made the excursion to Rochester, Rowell went to an attorney, William Watson, to ascertain if he had sufficient information to obtain a divorce. In what was to be advice that would change many lives, the attorney told him that he did not have enough support to win a divorce suit.

Rowell's mood shifted dramatically upon realizing the truth about his wife. Never an effervescent man he almost immediately became despondent. He began to have trouble focusing on his work. It got to the level that employees found him talking to himself. On more than one occasion Rowell was seen holding a picture of his wife saying, "She was such a pretty woman." The depression came on so suddenly and so completely that Rowell asked Palmer to buy out his interest in the factory. Rowell used as his reason for wanting out of the business a need for more time to consider his marital options and that while he was thinking he could not be active in the business. Palmer took the offer but made it clear that Rowell could buy his share back for the same amount at any time. Palmer was so fair in this transaction that he continued to pay Rowell, as an employee, the same amount as he had drawn as a partner in the business.

It was after Rowell's trip to Rochester and the meeting with the lawyer that he and Palmer set about planning to catch the duo in a compromising situation. The extent to which Palmer served as a catalyst in the conflict that would ensue would be debated for years. Some would say he was more than a catalyst in the plans and would be better described as the mastermind. So serious were the claims that it would be argued by many that Palmer "egged on" Rowell. In all discussions later, Palmer adamantly maintained that after the first four days of conversations about Jennie Rowell's meeting in Rochester, he took on a lesser role to Rowell. Palmer would say on numerous occasions that in the beginning he did start the conversations but after the fourth day he accepted a secondary role with Rowell initiating all the discussions.

With knowledge that his wife cared for another, the fate of the Rowells' two daughters in the event of a divorce was a concern for Newt. He puzzled over their care. He was bitter toward his wife, wishing that she would need to work to make enough money to live on. He could punish her if she were encumbered by the care of the girls. He feared that without the girls his wife would not have a problem making a living and would take up a party life. Something he believed she really wanted. At the same time if he had the girls he would be faced with the financial problem of maintaining their care

"The Plot"

Over the course of the next several weeks a plan was hatched that became known as "The Plot" in all the regional newspapers. This was a scenario agreed upon by Palmer and Rowell for trapping Lynch with Jennie. The two men took days concocting a scheme where they would catch Jennie and Lynch in a compromising position. The arrangements were developed over a period of several weeks and were modified numerous times before they were considered ready to be enacted. The discussions between the two men during September and October were so numerous that it was impossible to clearly determine who came up with each portion of the plan. What was agreed upon was that they felt that if they could catch Jennie and Lynch in a compromising position, public sympathy would be on Rowell's side. After the shooting, Palmer would argue in the newspapers that he kept telling Rowell that everything had to be done legally.

The plot fell into distinct sections. The first part was to provide an opportunity for the couple to meet. It was agreed that Rowell would use the excuse that he was leaving town on a sales trip to provide such an occasion. This was the easiest part of the plan as Rowell told his wife that he was going on a sales trip the last week in October. The second issue was location. Since Mrs. Rowell had demonstrated the previous August that she would go out of town to meet Lynch, it was important to establish where the couple would be together. It was Palmer's belief that Lynch had been in the Rowell home in Utica and would do the same if Rowell could get his new house finished. They also agreed that Rowell should not leave his wife any money, that way she could not go out of town to meet Lynch and he would have to come to Batavia. This was a time when people bought on credit. Everyone had an account at each of the stores. So if Rowell left his wife without money, it did not leave her in any way destitute. The final element was what to do with the couple when they were caught.

Several ideas were discussed but it was decided that Rowell would not leave town. Rather, he would stay hidden away in a retirement hotel in Batavia that overlooked the railroad station. While Rowell was in the hotel watching the incoming westbound trains, Palmer would have a key to the family post office box. Palmer would check the mail several times a day to see if Lynch was telling Jennie that he was coming to Batavia.

If Lynch played into their trap the two decided that Rowell would sneak into the house and hide in the cellar. From this vantage point he could hear what was going on upstairs without being detected. Rowell kept insisting that the front parlor would be a better location since he would have quick access to both the front door and stairs while still able to hear most conversations, except those in the kitchen. Palmer disagreed, holding that the possibility of being found was too great on the first floor. After he got in the house, Rowell would leave several windows unlocked so Palmer and his band could enter without a problem.

More important than where Rowell was to hide was what was to happen after the couple were alone. Rowell and Palmer both knew and feared Lynch. Palmer even said to Rowell that if he were to try to fight Lynch that he (Rowell) might very well find himself being thrown out an upstairs window without the benefit of it being opened first. They agreed on a group of three men they felt could be trusted, both for their strength and because if nothing were found, they would keep quiet about the whole affair. This band of men was going to make a great sport of Lynch by throwing him in the street naked. They would send his jewelry and other valuables to his moth-er. They would mail his clothes to the various newspapers in Utica. In the event the Batavia newspapers carried an article about the incident, a copy would be included with clothes. All in all, it would be quite the night.

***

Rowell prevailed upon his builder and was able to have the house finished the week before his planned trip. Several people came by the Rowells' house on the Sunday before the trip to see the new residence. Among those there that day were his new neighbor Charles Read and a local brewer, Hiram King. Both men noted separately how the normally thin and frail Rowell looked even weaker and pale. King thought Rowell was at the point of being considered emaciated. Those present that afternoon also thought Rowell was distracted. Rowell kept saying that the next day he would be going on a business trip out west. In the next breath he said he would be going to Washington, D.C., a point almost directly south. King said Rowell should not leave because Jennie was suffering from a bad cold. Rowell responded almost caustically, "Oh she'll get along fine."

***

Implementing the plot was one of the simple steps in the process. In the planning they had been concerned that Jennie would want to accompany Newt to the train station. Eventually Rowell decided that the best option was to leave very early in the morning so his wife would not want to escort him.

On Monday morning, Rowell got up early and went to the National Hotel where he registered under the name of H. S. Jones of Buffalo. Nervous and out of sorts, Rowell immediately told the clerk his real name but not his intentions nor the reason for the fictitious name. The manager of the hotel was happy for the money and never asked any questions. The National was perfectly located for Rowell's purposes. It was only separated from the train depot by a high board fence. From a room in the back Rowell could watch the train station to monitor if anyone was arriving (Lynch) or leaving (Jennie). If he desired he could climb the fence to look into the ladies lounge.

EARLY MAP OF BATAVIA
TRAIN TERMINAL AND NATIONAL HOTEL ARE BOTH VISIBLE
COURTESY OF GENESEE COUNTY HISTORIAN

From the vantage point of a window into the ladies waiting room, he could see if Jennie was awaiting a westbound train carrying Lynch.

The plot began to crumble and crack from the moment it was to be implemented. Rowell arrived at the National before the staff was on duty. The very nature of the hotel bothered Rowell. The National was a retirement hotel, having long passed its period of grace and charm. The dreary conditions at the hotel further contributed to Rowell's despair.

At ten that morning Palmer went to the National for his first visit with Rowell. Palmer assured Rowell he understood his difficulties with the environment but that he needed to stay in the hotel to maintain his vigil on the train station. They both knew this was probably the only place in Batavia where Rowell could go undetected and yet be able to do his own reconnaissance. Before Palmer left, Rowell produced a list of items he needed. Included on the list were his rubbers (needed for silence in the house), price book (so he could do work while he waited) and his revolver. Rowell told Palmer that he had a pistol in one of the drawers in his desk at the factory.

In the middle of the afternoon Palmer returned to the hotel where he found Rowell in the sitting room. Palmer had none of the request items his former partner had asked for that morning. Worse yet, Palmer told Rowell that there was no mail of consequence in the post box. The two visited for a while with Rowell complaining of how "tiresome" the atmosphere of the hotel was on his mission. Rowell added a good book to the list of items Palmer was to obtain.

Palmer's third visit that day was at nine in the evening. Palmer assured the anxious Rowell that he had been to the post office for the release of each mail. Despite their shared desire for a quick resolution to their case, no intimate mail had arrived. On this visit Palmer left Rowell with a book on the temperance movement in France and the revolver from the desk drawer. Curiously there was no discussion as to Rowell's desire or intent in having the pistol.

Palmer's fourth visit was on the morning of October 30th. On this occasion Rowell was in his room in the back of the hotel, looking down at the station. Yet again Palmer was forced to tell his confederate that he had no news for him. By now Rowell was beginning to seriously complain about his living arrangements. Rowell said he wished he had gone to Buffalo to wait, since at least he could have been doing some business and not just idling away his time. When Palmer left, Rowell had taken a position at the end of one of the halls where he could look down on the station. Rowell had a temperance book open on his lap.

At five that afternoon Palmer found Rowell in the bar of the hotel, standing near the side door. With a very different report to make, Palmer beckoned Rowell to join him in the privacy of the room. The two went swiftly to Rowell's room on the second floor. Palmer told Newt that they "had a piece of good luck." A telegram had just arrived at the box factory. According to Palmer the envelope was unsealed, so he read the message. The note, which was from Syracuse, was simple: "Will be up at 7:00." The message was signed Jennie Lowery. The conversation between Palmer and Rowell took less than five minutes with Palmer assuring Newt he would "gather the boys" and be at Rowell's house at nine that evening. They reviewed the plan that if Rowell was in the front salon he would leave a window open and signal his presence by having one curtain open and the other closed. If the curtains were not as planned, the men would enter through the basement.

After Palmer left, Rowell went downstairs to ask his landlord for some red pepper. The landlord, who was in the barroom lighting the gas lamps, said he did not have red pepper, but that he had some black pepper. Rowell declined the substitute pepper, asking instead for a woman's stocking. Suspicious, the innkeeper hedged on the stocking, asking its purpose. Rowell took a stone out of his pocket and showed it to his landlord, telling him he was going to use the stocking to hold the stone. When the innkeeper asked the purpose of his strange requests Rowell took a picture out of his pocket to show the man his wife's portrait saying, "I am after the ___ ___ ___ who is after this woman." The innkeeper told Rowell, "I don't know what you are up to and I don't want to be mixed up with anything you might do."

The landlord had made a mental note of how unnatural Rowell looked for his entire stay. He saw Rowell either very pale or flush. On several occasions Rowell was seen with tears in his eyes. The landlord would even go so far as to say Rowell had the look "of a mad dog."

The landlady, who was sick, and the hotel's one waitress were also both struck by Rowell's behavior. First, he ate less at the four meals that he had at the hotel than the landlady did at one. They were also struck by his inability to be attentive. They both noticed how Rowell was incessantly pacing and rarely spoke. He often had a book in his hands but they never saw him reading for more than a minute at a time. On that last Tuesday, after he heard about his wife's planned visitor, he had literally run out the west side of the building and just continued to run around the side yard. The waitress was so concerned she went after him. Without the support of the waitress, Rowell returned to the hotel. When he came inside Rowell went to his room where he stayed for less than ten minutes. At this point he left the National, never to return.

Unable to acquire red pepper or a stocking at his hotel, Rowell went to a small grocery store just opposite Court Street where a teenage clerk waited on him. For the second time Rowell found out that he could not get red pepper. Apparently, he now realized, red pepper would be hard to find, so he accepted black pepper, purchasing half a pound as a substitute. The boy thought it was strange that Rowell didn't want a bag but instead asked to have the pepper poured directly into his overcoat pocket.

Rowell then left the grocery store and went to a neighboring dry goods store. He asked the clerk for a lady's stocking. The clerk refused to break up a set but was willing to sell him a boy's sock. This was the sock that was found the next morning in the Rowells' salon with the stone wrapped and tied inside.

Newton Rowell was not the only family member busy making preparations that afternoon. Jennie became very busy after she received the telegram.

Mrs. Hiram King, Jennie's best friend in Batavia, was downtown shopping late in the afternoon of the shooting. The Kings had one child, a daughter, who was a great friend of the Rowell girls. To make the afternoon more pleasant for everyone, Mrs. King had dropped her daughter off at the Rowells' to play with her friends. After Jennie Rowell received the telegram informing her that Lynch was on his way, she had to rush to make preparations for her guest. One of the first things she did was to send the three girls to the King house with a note addressed to Mrs. King.

When Mrs. King arrived home she found the three little girls in the care of her maid. One of the girls produced the note. In it Jennie Rowell prevailed on her friend in a moment of need. She wrote how she was going to have an unexpected guest for tea, and needed Mrs. King's help supervising the girls. Jennie went on to say she had almost nothing in the house to serve and little time to shop.

Mrs. King gathered a basket with cake breads and some of the other items found later that night in the Rowell dining room. Since it would be unfit for a lady to be out later in the evening unescorted, Mrs. King told her maid to send her husband to collect her when he got home. Mrs. King then left the three little girls in the care of the maid and went to help out her neighbor.

When Mrs. King got to the Rowells' she found Jennie frantically trying to prepare tea. Mrs. King, who was by nature very sociable, found what was occurring intriguing. The two women sent for a neighbor, fourteen-year-old Mamie Showerman. Mamie was sent to the store with a note, made out by Jennie, to get additional food for dinner. Mamie picked up the oysters and the remainder of what had been seen on the table. The purchase was added to the Rowells' account at the store. At the same time, Jennie and Mrs. King set about preparing the house for

Johnson Lynch's arrival.

Of far more importance than the meal to these ladies of the Victorian Era, Jennie was not properly dressed to receive company. Mrs. King took over the kitchen, sending Jennie upstairs to get presentable for her guest.

Alone in the kitchen, and unaware of Rowell's presence in the salon, Mrs. King prepared the oysters and set the table. Since Hiram King did not come by the Rowells before Lynch arrived, Mrs. King sat down to tea with Jennie and her guest. When King did arrive Mrs. King had prevailed upon her husband to join them in tea but he had insisted on leaving. Readers may question why Mrs. King would ask her husband to stay at a function where a married woman was entertaining, in a private home, an unmarried gentleman caller. Perhaps Mrs. King wanted them to serve as chaperones. Or, the Kings may have been the other couple Palmer told Rowell about. The couple who had stayed at the hotel in Rochester the same night Jennie and Lynch had the previous August.

The Day After The Murder

Dr. Tozier conducted the autopsy in the front room of the Rowell residence. He found the track of one bullet that severed the major arteries near the heart and several veins in addition to doing damage to Lynch's lungs. So severe was the damage caused by the track of the ball that the doctor believed from the moment of the shot Lynch had only a few breaths before he would pass out and die. It was during these short breaths that all the blood came from his mouth and spilled across the foyer floor.

Dr. Tozier had heard the reports that Rowell had hit Lynch with the slingshot near the front door. The doctor was also present when the stone in the sock was found in the front salon. He checked Lynch's head for a wound severe enough to have been caused by the rock. There was a bruise but the doctor felt it was just as likely that the wound was from striking the floor-

board during the fall. The debate was irrelevant since the cause of death was the effects of the one bullet that had found its mark.

One of the factors that would influence the public's opinion of the case was the size of the two men involved. Lynch had not been eating properly for some time and weighed less than one hundred ten pounds. In contrast, Lynch was described by the doctors who did the autopsy as being Herculean in build, a trait that had obviously impressed Jennie.

The coroner found some interesting objects in Lynch's possession. The defense would make much of the six dollars in cash, a diamond shirt button and gold cufflinks. Only men who wanted to be perceived as being men of wealth wore jewelry such as a diamond collar button and gold cufflinks. Having only six dollars in his possession while out of town implied that Lynch was used to being able to live on credit – not expecting to be asked for payment. More interesting than his clothes or money were the five letters discovered in one of Lynch's jacket pockets. Two letters were from Jennie Rowell. The remaining three were from two other married women who lived in Utica.

When the coroner examined the body he also noted the way Lynch was dressed. At the time Lynch was running downstairs he did not have on his socks, shoes or suit jacket. His tie was still tight around his neck and his vest was still buttoned. His trousers were up but they were unlaced from the top down. A man unlaced his pants from the waist down if he wanted to take them off. If he needed to use the lavatory he unlaced his pants from the bottom up. Lynch's suit coat was found in the Rowells' bedchamber. At the time of his arrival the coroner noted that Mrs. Rowell's clothes were not disturbed.

The two letters written by Jennie Rowell were carried in all the newspapers covering the story. The correspondences that appear below are exactly as they appeared in the newspapers. The first letter has a misstatement. In all the newspapers it was remarked that Jennie had not seen Lynch in three years. In reality the amount of time was three months. This discrepancy was later noted, but whether the error was in Jennie's letter or in the way it was reported by the first newspaper is not clear. In any event the two had been together three months before in a hotel in Rochester.

Dearest John:

To say that I was glad to hear from you again does not express it. True it seems a long time since we saw each other, nearly three years ago. Only think how many things could happen in that amount of time. John, I miss you, O so much, and it is many sad days and lonesome days I have I assure you. We have been here two years yet I think of you just as fondly and as often as ever. Is it not strange of all the people we meet how few, how very few, we really care for. It isn't possible for me to meet you this week. R goes away soon to be gone four weeks. He is away nearly half the time. Was in Buffalo a week or so ago to do trading. We are fairly settled in our new home. You ask me what I find to amuse myself; I am going to study music this winter. There is some comfort in that. I am so fond of it. I want to see you very much. Have lots to tell you. Will drop you a line when R. goes and perhaps you can arrange to come here. I trust we shall see each other soon. With a world of love I remain your sincere friend,

Jennie
P.S. What has happened to Mrs. H. Have not heard from her in some time. Don't write until I write to you.
Batavia, Wednesday afternoon.

The second letter from Jennie Rowell is not much more detailed. However, it clearly shows that whatever promises Jennie had been making to her husband about not seeing Lynch were not meant to be kept.

Dearest John:

I am alone, - R. went away this morning. He will be absent two weeks or longer. Agreeable to you I should be glad to see you some evening this week, (say Thursday or Friday). Can you not get here at six and come up to teas soon afterwards. Will try and have the "chicks" in dreamland at seven. Let me hear from you soon. Will look for a letter Wednesday.

Affectionately,
Jennie L.

In addition to the letters in Lynch's pocket, there was a second significant discovery the day after the shooting. From the moment of the first reports out of the house, there had been a question as to the identity of the third party at the table. It took most of the day to prove who the person was and to get an explanation as to why the "mysterious third party" (Mrs. King) was in the house.

"The Dead Are At Rest."

The death of Johnson Livingston Lynch on Tuesday was just the opening tragedy for the remarkably wealthy and politically-connected Lynch/Johnson family that week. Lynch's funeral in Utica was on Friday. His body was just acclimating to its eternal resting place in Oakwood Cemetery when, on Saturday, his uncle and law office partner, Arthur B. (A. B.) Johnson, was found shot through the heart. To add to the scandals surrounding the family, A.B. had been found in a locked office by a young unmarried woman who had used a key to enter this most private of domains. The young woman's name was Lena Bender.

A. B. Johnson had left a handwritten note that was found later that day by his stepbrother, Craig Johnson, in a novel lying on the table in his sleeping chamber. The note read, "I have myself done this thing. Please ask no questions."

SOME OF THE UTICA CITIZENS WHO WERE INVOLVED IN NATIONAL POLITICS
WHEN THE CITY'S POWER WAS AT ITS ZENITH.

ROSCOE CONKLING
U. S. SENATOR AND SUPPORTER OF
PRESIDENT GRANT

HORATIO SEYMOUR
GOVERNOR AND CANDIDATE FOR
PRESIDENT 1868

WARD HUNT
SUPREME COURT JUSTICE
FATHER-IN-LAW OF A.B. JOHNSON

CONKLING'S MANSION IN UTICA

SEYMOUR'S GRAND HOME JUST NORTH OF UTICA

PICTURES COURTESY UTICA PUBLIC LIBRARY

To comprehend the magnitude of the deaths of Johnson and Lynch, one needs to understand the way the political stars had aligned over Utica in the late 1850s through 1870s. The involvement of Utica in national politics during this year can probably best be typified by the presidential election of 1868. The Democratic candidate was Horatio Seymour, a man who had previously served as mayor of Utica and governor of New York. Seymour ran unsuccessfully against Civil War General Ulysses S. Grant. Seymour received only 80 of the 294 electoral votes. To add intrigue to the political situation, one of Grant's chief advisors was New York Senator Roscoe Conkling. Like Seymour, Conkling was also a former mayor of Utica. The immense national power of this small upstate city becomes even more convoluted when one realizes that Conkling was Seymour's brother-in-law.

The power base neither began nor ended at this point. As a result of his support for Grant, Senator Conkling was able to entice the president to appoint another Utica native and yet one more previous mayor of Utica, Ward Hunt, to be a justice on the Supreme Court. The circle continues with Hunt's son-in-law, A. B. Johnson, who was Roscoe Conkling's chief advisor and the man behind the scenes. A. B. Johnson was the man who committed suicide. But even A. B. Johnson was not without a base. His great-grandfather was John Adams America's second president. His great-uncle, John Quincy Adams, had become close to Johnson's father. They were so close that John Quincy Adams visited the Johnson family in Utica while he was president.

The power of Utica did not start at this time. Alfred Conkling, father of Roscoe, had been a federal judge and the minister to Mexico. President John Adams' son-in-law, William Smith, the man who married the eldest daughter Abigail was a resident of neighboring Lebanon, New York.

U.S. Senator Roscoe Conkling, whose home was in Utica, was head of the state Republican Party. Conkling had long been a confidant of President Lincoln and later Grant. Conkling resigned from the Senate in 1881 in protest over some political appointments made by President Arthur. He may have had second thoughts about his rash action as he tried unsuccessfully to be reappointed to the Senate to fill his own seat. In the 1880s United States senators were still appointed by their state legislatures not by direct election of the people. Conkling did not lose his power just because he was out of office. He was offered the Supreme Court seat when Hunt retired due to a stroke in 1882. Conkling declined a seat on the bench and resumed his law practice, this time in New York City. Conkling continued to maintain a law office in Utica where, at the time of the shooting, he had an office immediately next to that of A. B. Johnson and Johnson Lynch.

The Adams Link

President John Adams and his wife, Abigail, had five children, four of whom reached adulthood. The children of two of their children, moved to Central New York but the Adams name did not follow. Both the Adams' oldest child, Abigail (Nabby), and their fourth child, Charles, have progeny who settled in the Mohawk Valley.

After the American Revolution John Adams was assigned as the minister to England. Knowing the stay in Europe would be a long one Adams wanted his family with him. Before she left with her mother for England, Nabby was considering marrying a lawyer from Quincy, Massachusetts. Concerned that she may be too young to marry, her parents talked Nabby into joining her mother on the trip to England, pleading that a separation from her young beau would be a good test of their relations. While she was in England her American friend became less interested in her and the two broke off their relationship. Conveniently, there was an American officer named William Steven Smith serving in London. Smith was the son of a very successful merchant in New York City and a veteran of the Revolutionary War. Nabby and William began seeing each other and married upon returning to the United States.

Being born into the right family may have been William's greatest success. He was a perpetual schemer, always trying to make it big on one investment rather than to establish himself in a profession. Often he was an embarrassment to the political family and his ability to support their only daughter was always a concern of the Adams'. After many tries at success William Smith and his family moved to Lebanon, New York.

The Adams fourth child, Charles, started out as the family member with the greatest natural prospects. He ended up being disowned by his father. Charles was a genuine charmer. As a boy, everyone he met both in America and Europe liked him. Before he was ten Charles suffered from a serious bout of smallpox which many thought would make him self-conscious. Instead he became even more engaging. Despite any scars he may have had from the pox, he was considered the best looking and most interesting of the Adams children. This charm came with a price. While he was at Harvard, those in the fast lane also sought his company. He was a great dancer and popular among the young women. His parents were concerned about his drinking and social habits, so much so that they did not even let him stay for commencement.

After Harvard, Charles settled in New York City where he studied law with the likes of Alexander Hamilton. Not particularly driven to hard work, Charles moved in with his sister Nabby and her husband. While living with them he fell madly in love with his brother-in-law's sister, Susan Smith. Susan, who was the youngest of the Smith children, was one year older than Charles. For two years they courted. Charles wanted to marry Susan but his parents objected, concerned that he could not afford a family and that his fast habits were still present. Without his parents' permission Charles and Susan Smith were married in September of 1795. They were twenty-five and twenty-six respectfully. As was predicted by Nabby, Susan seemed to have a calming effect on Charles. After one visit Abigail Adams said that if Charles were to return to his old ways it would not be Susan's fault. The union of

Charles and Susan resulted in two daughters, Abigail and Susanna.

At this time there was a serious concern about money among the Adams children. When John Quincy was leaving for Europe he left several thousand dollars in Charles' care to be invested conservatively. For over a year, the president and Abigail tried to find an accounting for this money. Finally in exasperation Charles said he had lent it to his brother-in-law (William Smith) to cover some bad debts. It was discovered that this account was not completely true. Charles had returned to drinking and the fast life. So serious was the problems with Charles that while John was president he were disowned his own son. Charles Adams died of cirrhosis of the liver in 1880 at the age of thirty. He left behind a wife and two children under the age of five.

Charles Adams' young widow, Susan (Smith), eventually moved to her brother's home outside Utica. Although only married five years and even with Charles being sick for much of that time the family did have two young daughters for her to care for. In 1814, their sixteen-year-old daughter, Abigail Louisa Adams, married an up-and-coming financial wizard, Alexander Bryan Johnson. Johnson was born in England but had migrated to the United States in 1801 to help in his father's retail business. The elder Johnson was a brilliant man known for having written books on philosophy and economics.

It was into this mini-aristocracy that Johnson Livingston Lynch, Jennie's lover, was born. There is an expression that a business is either growing or shrinking it can never stay exactly the same. The same may be true for a family. Johnson Lynch's heritage could be traced back to the Mayflower. He was descended from one of the three men who drafted the Declaration of Independence. His grandfather and father were self-made men, deriving their fortunes in banking and finance. His grandfather and uncles were considered men of letters, having the ability to quote great literature and having published their own thesis. His uncles were lawyers and judges. He knew men who had been mayors, governor,

THE LYNCH FAMILY HOME
THIS HOUSE STILL STANDS ON PLANT STREET IN UTICA

Supreme Court justice and another who had run for president. He was friendly with a senator who had been the county district attorney at the age of twenty-one. Now at thirty Lynch had no similar success to look back upon or any vehicle that would carry him to any significant position of power. He was in effect only successful as the family playboy.

Lynch was a lawyer who was technically in the same office as his uncle A. B. Johnson. By this time he was not practicing law. He had entered the stock market to become a broker in the firm of his friend C. H. Yates.

The Legacy Repeated

It is worth noting the parallels between Johnson Lynch and his great-grandfather, Charles Adams. Abigail Adams, the wife of the president, worried about her son Charles because he was an exquisite dancer and a favorite of the girls. She was also concerned about his disposition, which she said would render him more susceptible to female attachments. John Adams spoke about Charles as, "a madman possessed of the devil." Adams used such terms as "rake", "beast", and a "reprobate who shall be punished" when talking of his son. Ultimately, and with much regret later, John Adams had been forced to say, "I renounce him." Shortly before his death Abigail said of Charles, "vice and destruction have swallowed him up … All is lost – poor, poor unhappy man." She went on to say, "God knows what is to become of him." Abigail referred to Charles as "a life, which might have been made valuable to himself and others." On one occasion she said, "He was no man's enemy but his own." Both Johnson Lynch and his great-grandfather Charles Adams were the most promising members of their family. Both men succumbed to the social lifestyle handed to them by their families and enhanced by their own personality. Both men at thirty died as result of their choices.

The Mentor

A. B. Johnson was in political terms what is considered the classic man behind the man. Although never holding a significant political office, Johnson had been at all the most important events in the preceding five years. He had been a member of the New York Republican delegation to the 1876 National Convention in Cleveland where Hayes was nominated for president. In 1881 he was rumored to have been the dealmaker behind the selection of Thomas Platt to serve out the term of his political mentor, Roscoe Conkling. Johnson had been appointed to the position of claims agent for both the Army and the Navy. He had been selected by President Arthur to inspect one section of the Northern Pacific Railroad. His father-in-law, Ward Hunt, had served rather benignly on the Supreme Court of the United States. Johnson's brother, Alexander, had been on the New York State Court of Appeals (New York's highest court) until he resigned to accept a federal judge position. His brother was General Charles Johnson who served with distinction in the Union Army during the Civil War.

Arthur B. Johnson (called A. B. to differentiate him from his brother Alexander) appeared to have it all. He lived in one of the nicest houses on one of the best streets in Utica. He was born of money and rumor had it that he had made many strategic investments that had made him even wealthier. He was considered a successful lawyer. The community was in shock as they wondered why he suddenly took his own life.

Johnson was a model of the Victorian Gentleman. He was proud of his mind. He could quote the Bible, poetry and Shakespeare. He was talented in law, literature, art and what in many ways was the new art of the 1800s ? science. He was a painter and sculptor, having become interested on a European trip. He could read Latin and Greek and was considered a French scholar. *The Utica Herald* said of him in an obituary many will envy:

He was able to repeat, almost literally from beginning to end, several of the plays (Shakespeare's), which were his delight and study. In the business quality Mr. Johnson was marvelously endowed. His executive capacity, on occasions, which called for it into exercise, seemed almost unlimited. He dispatched work rapidly, managed men, kept control of various threads, and was cool, quick and nervy in forming important decisions. Socially, he was always the center of brilliant, entertaining and instructive conversation. Widely informed, gifted in wit, and affluent of speech, his company was eagerly sought by a large circle of friends, who were bound to

him by many traits of character which were admirable, and the memory of which will outlive the memory of his faults.

Johnson had an imposing, domineering manner, which was softened by his good-natured wit and genial manners. He was popular among his friends. He was a large landowner with much of the property on the east side of Utica among his holdings. This is part of the property on which so many of the mills were later constructed. He owned interest in railroads and mines. Among his assets were shares in a mine in Montana. Before investing in this particular mine A. B. had visited it. In the days of Indian unrest he had returned six hundred miles to Salt Lake City with just his

LAWYER JOHNSON'S DEAD SHOT.

THE UNCLE OF JOHNSON L. LYNCH, WHO WAS KILLED BY AN OUTRAGED HUSBAND AT BATAVIA, COMMITS SUICIDE AT UTICA, N. Y., IN A FIT OF REMORSE AND RUM.
THE SENSATIONAL SEQUEL OF A SENSATIONAL TRAGEDY

ARTIST ILLUSTRATION OF LENA BENDER DISCOVERING THE BODY OF A. B. JOHNSON.
NOTE: THE ARTIST WANTED TO ESTABLISH THE MOOD FOR A DEN DESIGNED FOR DEBAUCHERY BY INCLUDING THE PICTURE ON THE WALL AND THE STATUE.
THIS GRAPHIC APPEARED IN *THE NATIONAL POLICE GAZETTE.*

driver. This act was all the more defining of his personal character as it was in the winter and he had to dress in animal skins to keep from freezing to death. He considered himself a chemist, having a lab in his office. Johnson also had controlling interest in the tunnel under the Hudson River at New York City and owned many shares of the new Edison Electric Company.

At age fifty-eight Johnson was fortunate to be somewhat portly. In this time to have a slight paunch was to demonstrate to the world your success. The vast majority of men had to work at hard, laborious jobs. Pictures of men from this period show that they were, as a group, thin. The common laborer's income was so low he had to struggle to have enough to put food on his family's table. In contrast, Johnson's paunch showed he could afford rich food and did not have any work that would be considered exercise. On the negative side, there were also many reports that A. B. would go on drinking sprees.

When the first reports of his suicide came out it appeared that Johnson showed his success and status in at least one other way. For some time it had been rumored around Utica that he and his private secretary, Lena Bender, had been more than just employee and employer. It is difficult to get a true handle on the relationship between Johnson and Lena Bender. Among the first set of rumors was one that Johnson and Lena, when visiting other cities, would register in hotels as husband and wife. For those who delighted in such rumors it was noted that the two always traveled on separate trains. There was also gossip that A. B. Johnson would visit her house in daylight. Visiting Lena was less of a social faux pas than might be at first perceived as Lena lived with her parents and brother, John. Her father, Valentine Bender, owned a hotel which had a bar and restaurant. The family's hotel was just across the Mohawk from Utica in a hamlet called Deerfield. She is described in some reports as an uninteresting girl while in others she was attractive. At the same time that the ruse between Johnson and Lena was supposedly being maintained, others told of seeing them rowing upon the Mohawk

River, a very romantic activity. In either case, in the early reports she was reputed to wear expensive jewelry and clothes – both of which were believed to be beyond the resources of her or her family.

A.B. Johnson's wake was held at his home. There was a report that Lena tried to get into the wake and was stopped at the door. She denied this accusation saying that she and her brother were

THE JOHNSON FAMILY MANSION
ON GENESEE STREET IN UTICA
THE HOUSE WAS TAKEN DOWN AND REPLACED BY
THE SAVINGS BANK.
PICTURE COURTESY OF UTICA PUBLIC LIBRARY

just out for a walk to help relieve her of her grief.

The Johnson brothers, as a group, appear to have been close to the Bender family. The evening before he committed suicide, Lena's brother had walked A. B. to his office from the Bender's hotel. After A. B.'s funeral his brother General Charles Johnson called on Lena and her family to express his condolences, not something that would be expected for a mistress.

Mrs. Johnson was reported to have accepted her husband's life-style out of pride and to keep up an image within the social circle. When the news of Johnson's death reached Mrs. Johnson and her children the family broke down in tears.

The death of Johnson Lynch had had a profound effect on A.B. Johnson. He allegedly went on one of his drinking sprees. He was so distraught that he could not even attend his favorite nephew's funeral, spending the time instead at Lena Bender's father's establishment. Throughout the days following the news of Lynch's death, Johnson had slipped deeper and deeper into depression. Much of these four days was spent with Lena where he was often heard repeating the same phrase about Lynch, "Poor boy, poor boy." True to his intellectual capacity at more rational moments during his period of mourning he was said to have quoted the Bard, "If it were done when 'tis done, then well it were done quickly." And, "Oh, death where is thy sting." On one occasion A. B. came upon a group of men discussing his nephew's death. He quoted Corinthians 13, "For we know in part and prophesy in part." He felt that the men did not listen, intent instead on their own interpretation of what had occurred. To Lena, Johnson put his feelings about his effectiveness with these men as, "I might as well have recited it to a stone."

Johnson told Lena that he feared that he was having a breakdown. In recent years both his brother and brother-in-law, James McDonald, had died in asylums and Johnson feared the same fate. Lena was so sure that Johnson was contemplating suicide that she hid his handgun. In retaliation for her protection he told her that the best method for suicide was to push a penknife into the jugular vein, being sure to sever the artery.

In the days that followed A. B.'s death, Lena Bender was able to get several newspapers to paint a different picture of her and her relationship with Johnson. These reports followed General Johnson's visit to her family's home. With this dramatic show of support she set about telling of her connection to Johnson from a professional point of view. Suddenly, she was not being portrayed as a paramour but rather as a confidential clerk. A more accurate description could be a calculating woman climbing to the height of political power by attaching herself to the arm of an influential man. This after all was thirty-five years before women could vote, let alone hold office. She was now rumored to be the source of the "cipher dispatch" of the 1880 campaign. She claimed to be behind some of Johnson's financial investments, which she said left his estate valued at over $5,000,000.

Arthur B. Johnson's funeral was a very private affair. No public notice was given and only members of the immediate family and a few close associates were present. It is worth noting two of the pallbearers. One was former U. S. Senator Roscoe Conkling and another was the son of William Seward, Lincoln's secretary of state. The senior Seward had suffered an attempt on his life the same night that Lincoln was assassinated.

Weeks later a report came out that Arthur Johnson was not as successful as at first believed. Johnson was the executor of his brother-in-law, James McDonald's, estate. At the time of his death McDonald was believed to be worth about three-quarters of a million dollars. The accounting for the real estate and liquid part of his assets was perfect. However when they tried to find some of the bonds and stocks that were said to belong to the estate, they were missing. Now Johnson was being painted as a defaulter. There was still almost $400,000 worth of real estate left so Johnson's sister would not live in poverty, but there was a serious question as to what had happened to the rest of the money.

On the day Arthur Johnson's body was discovered, Newt Rowell was formally committed to jail pending the outcome of the grand jury. The grand jury of Genesee County was scheduled to hear the case the next week.

November 4th

It was a full five days before Jennie Rowell hired a hack to take her and her mother, Mrs. Luce, to visit Rowell at the village jail. Jennie had covered her hat and face with a heavy veil that made her harder to see but more intriguing to watch. The national connections that this trial put forward made every reporter from the area, and many people with no sound reason, want to visit Rowell. He did not want to see anyone he did not know, thinking that they looked upon him like "an animal in a menagerie." To avoid a problem they developed a special system to admit visitors into the building to visit with the prisoner. Visitors were required to wait at the building door until the deputy on duty could check to see if Rowell would accept the visitor.

Rowell was shocked when asked by the deputy if he wanted to see his wife responding, "Before you let her in –" his thought ended mid-sentence. Regaining his self-confidence he continued, "but is she alone?" Told that her mother had accompanied Jennie, Rowell said, "Well let them in." When the deputy opened the outside door Mrs. Luce refused to enter, returning instead to the carriage.

The building that housed her husband so intimidated Jennie that as she and the jailor walked toward the space occupied by Rowell, she was forced to lean on the deputy for support. The jail did not have individual cells and those inside moved about with relative impunity. When she actually got to the area where Rowell was housed, she started to faint. She was only held from falling to the floor by the outstretched compassionate arms of her husband. When they were alone the Rowells conversed for half an hour. Jennie's sobs could be heard clearly by the jailor who, to give the couple some privacy, waited in a separate area.

When Jennie finished her visit she left the building. At the carriage she told her mother that Rowell wanted to see her. At first Mrs. Luce refused saying, "I don't want to go in there."

"But he wants to see you," her daughter beseeched her mother.

Eventually Jennie was able to prevail upon her mother to enter the jail. Mrs. Luce only met with Rowell for a few minutes. When the two women left they took the hack to the house on Bank Street, avoiding the main streets.

After a couple of weeks in the jail Rowell was given, as his residence, the entire section of the building that was supposed to house women prisoners. This section was rarely used, so Rowell was allowed to have personal furniture moved from his house to his new and hopefully temporary residence. Rowell spent his time reading books and collecting any newspapers that carried articles about what had happened on that infa-mous night, or any articles with features about persons connected to the case. He had numerous visitors, often as many as thirty in a single day. He also spent time with the rest of the men who were locked up. He gained a new respect for these men thinking that they each had a story and that they were far less intimidating than they looked.

Newt Rowell and Jennie Luce

The Rowells were married September 8, 1875. Jennie's father and Newt had worked for the same company (N. C. Newell) in Clayville. Jennie's father was impressed enough with the energy of Newt that he introduced the young man to his daughter. Their courtship had been strange from the very beginning. Jennie would tell others that when Newt came round the house she was unsure whether Newt wanted her or her sister's company until he actually asked for her hand. After the wedding the couple moved several times once, in 1877, to Howard Street in Utica. Howard Street, at the time, was lined with brick homes that attracted the up-and-coming young middleclass families. In the early years Jennie had two daughters, Edna and Clara, thirteen months apart. Newt proved to be a devoted father. When the Rowells entertained in the evening Newt would often put his daughters down for the night, leaving his wife to amuse their guest. In Victorian times this would be considered, at the very least, an unusual behavior.

Newt Rowell was the oldest of three children. His brother, George, was a printer in Utica. His sister, Julia, a teacher at the high school, was still single and living with her father. His mother, Elvia, died at the age of thirty-one. Newt was only eight at the time of his mother's death. His father remarried and Newt's stepmother was a presence at many times during the events that followed.

When he was an adolescent Newt Rowell was besieged by nightmares. The exact cause was not accounted for, but he was reported to have

THE OLD GALLOWS
THESE WERE THE GENESEE COUNTY GALLOWS
THAT SOME THOUGHT ROWELL MAY HAVE TO FACE
COURTESY OF HOLLAND PATTON MUSEUM

similar dreams even as an adult. One cause may have been stress, as these dreams were more frequent during the trial.

The Grand Jury

It was the third week in November when the grand jury finally met. It is believed that their ultimate charge of manslaughter in the first degree was a compromise. It was reasoned that the opinions of the members of the grand jury covered the entire spectrum. Many on the jury felt that Rowell acted within his legal and definitely moral rights and should go free; while others felt that a charge of murder in the first degree was appropriate. From what could be learned about the grand jury's deliberations, the manslaughter charge was a

middle ground and the best the district attorney could orchestrate. First-degree manslaughter was defined as the killing of a person with a deadly weapon in an act of passion. It differed from murder in the first degree because of the element of intent. In manslaughter the person did not intend to bring on the death while the first-degree charge would mean that the victim's death was the desired outcome from the outset.

The same grand jury failed to bring a charge of bigamy against the farmer, mentioned at the beginning of this story, who was arrested the night before Lynch was shot. Other than the inscription on the letters saying dearest husband and signed your wife no evidence of a wedding could be found. The farmer was left to deal with his wife and divorce lawyers. We will never know if he would have preferred jail.

When Rowell was formally arraigned on the charge of manslaughter on November 17th his father, brother and sister were all present. After hearing the charge Rowell was asked to enter a plea. In a loud clear voice he responded, "Not guilty." No date was set for the trial nor was the issue of his bail discussed.

On November 22nd, Jennie Rowell had had enough of Batavia. She took the morning train bound for Utica. There she would go by carriage to her parents' home in Clayville, a rural community south of Utica. Word of her trip spread quickly and groups of onlookers were present at each train stop, hoping for a glimpse of the "notorious woman" whose deceit was causing such a national sensation. Jennie was wearing a heavy blue veil throughout the trip, causing most of those who came to see her at the various train stations along the way to leave disappointed.

When she arrived in Utica several of her acquaintances were at the station to meet her. Encouraged by the demonstration of support shown at the station, she actually chatted with several people. She stayed at the station long enough for some of those gathered to be able to claim they had caught a quick look at her.

By mid-November Jennie Rowell's life-style was more on trial than her husband's crime. *The Utica Globe* reported that at the trial the defense was going to seek testimony tracing Jennie's behavior back to the day the Rowells moved to Utica. The defense was going to put before the court a record of "illicit intercourse" between Jennie, Lynch, other men and even some other women. It was said the they were interviewing waiters, innkeepers and Jennie's friends, looking for individuals who had attended picnics, private parties and had gone on excursions to out of the way resorts. *The Globe* went on to say that those who feared they might be summoned were moving out of Utica so fast those in their social circle wondered what would become of the city's young people. There were even rumors that Jennie Rowell's adventures would impact other cities besides just Utica and Batavia including Syracuse, Rochester and Auburn. It was rapidly becoming apparent that having social connections to Jennie were not as simple or limited as they first appeared.

Following the shooting Jennie Rowell tried to avoid any interviews. This did not keep her name out of the newspapers, nor did it keep the rumor-hungry reporters from finding stories about her. She was described in *The Batavia News* as "bright and pretty, a good talker and to all outward appearances well behaved." They told how she appeared to her neighbors to be a caring mother and resourceful wife. Her two girls were naturally attractive and Jennie had done well at keeping them stylishly dressed. Of most importance to Calvinistic New England, Jennie had to maintain her house and children without the aid of a maid.

There was an interview that was printed in *The Batavia News* that presented what had happened to Jennie in a more favorable light. Exactly who was interviewed and whether Jennie had agreed in some way to have the person be interviewed is not clear but in this one article Jennie comes off as someone who made some wrong turns not the blatant harlot she was painted in most newspapers. *The Batavia News* said that the unnamed person they interviewed was a female friend of Jennie's. The friend had visited Jennie while she was staying in the hotel in Batavia before she left for Clayville. This unnamed supporter was said to have known Jennie for years. According to the associate, Jennie and Newt Rowell had moved to Utica shortly after their marriage. To a rural girl like Jennie, Utica offered a big city life-style. For the first time she was introduced to quality theater, the orchestra, and lectures. Even more significant were the social parties. It was the fascination with this social life that proved Jennie's downfall.

One of Jennie's neighbors, some said it was the lady who lived in the other half of the duplex in which the Rowells lived, was living a duplicitous life. When the Rowells moved to Utica they lived in a stylish duplex suitable for a professional family not born to money. On the outside of the house was a neighbor who on the outside was respectable and socially acceptable. It was later learned that the lady's funds were obtained from many of Utica's men of wealth. With Newt traveling almost half the time Jennie had prolonged periods when she was on her own. According to Jennie's friend, the former neighbor literally seduced Jennie into a social life and life-style that navigated the course of events that happened on October 30th. This neighbor visited Jennie almost exclusively when Newt was away on sales trips. Alone and lonely, the neighbor engaged the attractive Jennie in intimate conversations. The neighbor had little trouble convincing the naive Jennie that Rowell was not a good lover, pointing out his lack of affection and how his lovemaking was "matter of fact."

In time Jennie started taking rides and going on picnics with her neighbor and some of her male associates. Exactly how many of these rides Jennie went on and with how many men was not printed in any of the reports. This void left the gossip-hungry moralist ample space to speculate. It was on one of these outings that Jennie met Johnson Lynch. To Jennie, Lynch was everything that Rowell wasn't. Lynch was a sharp dresser, highly articulate, good looking and born to a high place in life. Perhaps most important he was a good dancer. Lynch traveled in the circles that she believed Rowell never would. It was easy for the unsophisticated Jennie to fall in love with such a man. Not to be taken for a woman seeking financial favor, Jennie pointed with pride to the fact that Lynch never gave her gifts and she never accepted any money from him. Either of these would have lowered her status even more.

Although seeming to enjoy her companionship, Lynch never expressed love for Jennie. However, it was in the company of Jennie that Lynch reportedly lowered his guard. He shared with her his perception of himself. Lynch told Jennie that even though he may appear a man who had all his earthly needs met in reality had a very different opinion of himself. While on the outside he was the epitome of success, inside he felt that he had failed at every endeavor he attempted. In their most intimate of moments Lynch had confided to Jennie that he was tired of his life.

Jennie's friend ended the *News* interview with two very interesting anecdotes that told how Jennie was feeling. The friend told of how, when she saw Jennie just hours before, she had expressed her feeling for Lynch, "Oh, if only I had told him not to come here!" Jennie had said before she broke down. Jennie was more concerned about Lynch than Rowell or her children. Her friend asked Jennie the question on everyone's mind, "Would she ever live with Rowell again if he would take her back?" Jennie's response was, "No indeed. Do you suppose that I could ever live with that man again? How could he be so cruel? I shall always think of John as he looked up at me from the floor that awful night. I never can forget that look. I am going back to Clayville to live but I fear I shall go crazy."

The month of November 1882 was spent with everyone in Utica and Batavia expressing an opinion about the events and the appropriate punishment. To most, especially those in Batavia, Rowell should simply be released. Others, those who believed that morality should be legislated, were using this case as an example of why the state needed to pass a bill against adultery. Ministers used the opportunity to preach the certain moral destruction of families if women did not remain in the home. Like every other event of national interest and moral failure this was the topic of daily conversation.

One article in *The Utica Observer* summarized the gossip surrounding Jennie Rowell and her associates. Apparently, when they lived in Utica, it was common to see carriages parked under the trees near the Rowell home. When one looked closely they would see inside these carriages some of the "well known young men." It was reported that Mrs. Jennie Rowell would often be seen inside these carriages. The newspaper said that she was one of several young women led into a life of "disgrace and illicit alliance" by a beautiful woman with an "insinuating address." In a later interview William Palmer would put the name Mrs. Williams to this description. This article also supports many of William Palmer's claims about Jennie as an adulterous wife.

The two levels on which the people of Batavia knew Jennie Rowell fascinated the Rome *Sentinels* reporter. It was said that her only friend in Batavia was the cunning little Mrs. King who would never tell all that she knew. At the same time the reporter felt that it was amazing how many professional men were suddenly being called out of Batavia just as the trial was to begin. In this reporter's words, "She must have been, to say the very least, a very sociable woman." In fact when the news first broke it was believed that it was a local man who was shot. The reporter continued, "The friends of various men breathed easier when they saw them alive." Apparently if one kept their ears open they would hear many men congratulate each other on not being the one found on the floor of the Rowells' foyer.

From a Victorian moral standpoint, there was one positive to all these claims coming out of Utica. Suddenly young men, who were in the practice of leaving their young wives alone in the evening while they went to their various clubs, were now staying home to protect their hearths.

***

As the trial approached speculation about who

would be called as a witness and what extraneous information would be shared circulated based on opinion not fact. As the month of January wore on lawyers from both sides acknowledged that they would not be calling any more witnesses than absolutely necessary to win the case. This disclosure left open the fascinating possibility that either or both Jennie and Newt Rowell would testify. The lawyers' statements did close the prospect of this trial being one of the great sex scandals of the Victorian era. The people who bought the daily newspapers were ready to read of the moral decay of those of power and wealth.

A week before the trial *The Batavia News* again interviewed Rowell. The reporter was impressed by how positively Rowell spoke about Jennie's parents. Newt respected the Luces and how they had raised their daughter. He expressed quite different feelings about the Lynchs. Rowell told the reporter that Johnson Lynch lived fast and was popular with "the boys."

Rowell shared a story about a fellow prisoner with the reporter. The man had been arrested for having escaped from the jail in Brockport. When Rowell asked the man why he had been in jail originally he responded in a gruff voice, "I killed something." The man looked at the windows in Rowell's area as if to consider his escape options in Batavia then left. Later that day the same man returned and asked Rowell to join him in a card game. Rowell declined, saying he didn't gamble. The man then asked Rowell for a drink. Rowell assured the man he didn't drink either. The man was astonished saying, "Don't play cards and don't drink. Then what the ___ are you in jail for?" It wasn't really a question but rather demonstrated the moral dilemma of the Victorian Era that all crimes could be traced to either alcohol or gambling. The man had concluded his conversation by assuring Rowell that he was addicted to drink and usually made a fool of himself while on a spree.

It came out just before the trial that "the boys," as Rowell had referred to them, had visited ex-Senator Conkling in New York City to see if he would join the prosecution team. Conkling begged off, saying that the case belonged to the prosecutor elected by the people. It can only be speculated on as to what impact Conkling would have had on the outcome of the trial had he joined the team. No doubt the presence of a man of his national renown would have made this case even more of a spectacle.
***

Three days before the trial the players were all gathered in Batavia. Rowell's attorneys, Judge William Sutton of Utica and William Watson of Batavia, met each morning with Rowell at the village jail. After their meeting, the lawyers would go to Sutton's room at the Washburn House. Sutton's room had been converted into a makeshift law office filled with books and piles of papers.

Jennie Rowell did not want to stay in the house on Bank Street and was staying at a different hotel than her husband's attorneys. Her attorney, S. S. Morgan, assured the reporters that Jennie would not be a voluntary witness. He then took the reporters into Jennie's room where she made one of her few public statements. She told the reporters that she suffered daily from headaches and needed "absolute rest" – a euphemism for bed rest. She assured reporters that she had received numerous letters of support both from friends and strangers. These letters had helped her fight the depression brought on by the events of late October. In the two months since her friend had been interviewed Jennie had mellowed in her stand with respect to living with Rowell again. This time she said, "Who can tell what the future will be?"

The Interview

During the trial *The Batavia Times* carried an interview that was attributed to Jennie Rowell in a section called *The Spirit of the Times*. What had happened to make Jennie break her silence with the press was a bit of a misrepresentation. At the trial it would come out that the reports that Mrs. King brought the makings for the dinner with Lynch was not totally correct. In fact a young neighborhood girl had been sent to get many of the items. This young girl's father, a part-time reporter for the *Times*, visited Jennie when she returned to Batavia from Clayville for the trial. At their meeting Jennie thought she was talking to a friend and made some comments. What appeared in the *Times* article was a damnation of Palmer. In making clear her position, Jennie was reported to have said of Palmer that he is "one of the most contemptible, treacherous, black hearted wretches that ever disgraced the name of man-hood." In the article Jennie claimed that Palmer did not want to reform her but rather to "become a partner in my sin." In the article Jennie claimed that Palmer had done all he could to smear her reputation in Batavia. The article closed with an assurance by Jennie that she was sorry for her indiscretions and wanted to lead a virtuous life in the future.

The next day a reporter from *The Batavia News* interviewed Jennie and found her angry about the article in the *Times*. Jennie said that she was never interviewed. But she did take this opportunity to correct some of the statements attributed to her.

The following day the reporter for the *Times* swore a statement before a notary that the contents of the interview were the result of his discussion with Jennie. After the trial was over the *Times* admitted that the article was made up but argued that it expressed Jennie's feelings.

This incident showed the extremes that the newspapers would go to grab a headline that was theirs alone. It also shows that to be quiet, as Jennie was, can be more compelling than to talk to the press, as Palmer would after his testimony.

The Trial

It was early in the evening of Saturday, January 19th, when Edward Newton "Newt" Rowell left the jail where he had been confined since the previous October 30th. After almost three months of incarceration his attorneys had quietly petitioned for bail. The district attorney knew that their reason was to have Rowell close by, rather than having to visit him in jail, therefore, he did not object. After the presidents of two local banks signed bonds, Rowell was released in a very unceremonial moment.

That evening the train from Utica was an hour late in getting to Batavia. This actually worked to Rowell's advantage, as he was able to be at the station to greet those who arrived on that train. Among the passengers were Rowell's father, stepmother, uncle, sister and, most important to him, his daughters, Edna and Clara. Rowell had not seen his children since the morning before the death of Lynch. After an emotional greeting the parties went back to the Rowell home on Bank Street. The family all gathered in the place where the shooting had occurred. These members of the Rowell family would stay in the Bank Street house for the duration of the trial.

Even as the trial began everyone in Batavia knew that this would be one of the community's most famous events. Batavia for the next two weeks was the place to be.

Reporters were present from Rochester, Buffalo and Utica. The newly-formed Associated Press was also represented. Reports of the shooting had appeared in *The New York Times* and *The Nation Police Gazette*. The magnitude of the story was clear in just the sales of *The Batavia News*. Prior to the incident *The Batavia News* printed about 1,700 copies of each edition. Starting with the day after the shooting the *News* printed more than 5,000 copies. In a single day their circulation tripled. With the sale price of one cent a copy the newspaper suddenly had a daily revenue of fifty dollars.

As noted earlier, attorneys William C. Watson of Batavia and Judge William Sutton of Utica conducted Newt Rowell's defense. Watson was the same lawyer who had advised Rowell that he did not have sufficient evidence to file for a divorce. Watson was born in 1837 in Pembroke, a community not far form Batavia. He began the practice of law in 1865. He was elected district attorney twice and had finished in this capacity

W. C. WATSON
DEFENSE ATTORNEY
COURTESY HOLLAND PATTON MUSEUM

SAFFORD NORTH
DISTRICT ATTORNEY
COURTESY HOLLAND PATTON MUSEUM

shortly before the trial began. Sutton was brought in for his skill and his connections to the players from Utica. Rowell and his father had known Sutton in Utica. Sutton had a colorful courtroom presence. As he questioned a witness he would put his hands in his pants pockets. Many were impressed that it looked like he would reach down into the pockets so deeply that he appeared to be scratching his knees. However clumsy and awkward his appearance, Sutton was brilliant in his field and proved capable of thinking on his feet. The team proved to be excellent as Watson proved to be Sutton's equal in the courtroom.

The prosecution was lead by District Attorney Safford North, joined by Judge Lucius Bangs of Buffalo. North celebrated his thirtieth birthday just after the trial ended. In the days when lawyers were schooled by veteran attorneys rather than by colleges, North had begun his legal training under Judge Bangs. Bangs was considered a true legal authority capable of conversing on even the smallest point of law. It is interesting

to note that North concluded his legal training under William Watson, the defense attorney.

Judge Haight of Buffalo was only thirty-eight and the youngest judge on the bench when he was selected to preside in this case of national interest. He was tall and thin, with the habit of standing unusually straight. His long black hair and mustache were always well groomed. When an objection occurred during the trial Haight had the trait of hearing both sides of the argument

BATAVIA TRAIN STATION
THE FIRST PLACE IN BATAVIA EXPERIENCED BY
LYNCH AND LAWYERS.
COURTESY HOLLAND PATTON MUSEUM

34

then asking the court reporter to reread the question. He would then sustain the objection or let the witness answer. The reporters all felt he was incredibly just and deserving of presiding in a case of this magnitude. The judge's only weakness was his commute. Judge Haight's railroad commute from Buffalo to Batavia would be a problem on two different occasions.

It took almost two days and one hundred and nineteen potential jurors to select a panel. The bulk of the jurors (eight) claimed to be farmers. This may very well have been the case. In Western New York the convergence of Victorian and Calvinist values were at their peak in 1883. Under these social rules being a farmer was considered a noble and humble occupation. If they lived on a farm, it was common in this era for people to refer to themselves as farmers even when they were doctors or lawyers. Therefore, we will never know exactly how many members of the jury were actually farmers.

There was never much contention about what happened in the Rowell house on the evening of October 30th. What was at issue during the trial was:

- Rowell's state of mind at the time the shot was fired
- His motive in going to the house
- Whether Rowell felt threatened by Lynch and therefore shot the gun in self-defense
- Whether Rowell was insane at the moment the shot was fired
- Lynch's character, especially as it compared to Rowell's character and
- To an even greater extent the rules under which Victorian society operated.

In effect the principle question being asked was, did a husband have the right to shoot his wife's lover if he finds the two in bed together? Rowell had gone to his house armed with an offensive weapon in the slingshot and an even more uncompromising weapon in the pistol. True, he did have a "plot" that included only limited violence. He had brought along a pocketful of pepper to handle a lesser situation, yet gave up on the pepper after only a few seconds and drew on the most offensive weapon in his arsenal.

The Prosecution

One of the biggest problems the prosecution had was the charge of manslaughter, which had been brought down by the grand jury. The district attorney had wanted a charge of first-degree murder where they could show planning and deliberate intent. The manslaughter charge meant they had to show passion and anger and not intent. The manslaughter charge was a problem because "The Plot" was already well known by everyone in the region. The plot would have helped prove a charge of murder in the first-degree since it showed the husband was aware of his wife's behavior, but would hinder a successful charge where passion was a required element. The prosecution knew they had to acknowledge that Rowell was hidden in the house for an hour and a half while Lynch was present. He had come armed with lethal weapons and was aware that he had confederates who were to arrive and help him gather evidence and punish the transgressor. If they leaned too heavily on the anger pushing him they would open the door to a plea of insanity. Thus, the prosecution went into the case with right in the legal sense on their side and virtually a whole community emotionally opposed to them.

When Palmer was finally put on the stand it was standing room only in the court. The spectators wanted to hear from the man who had been in on the planning of events that night. They wanted to resolve for themselves the extent of blame that belonged to the defendant and the amount that should be shared by his former partner.

Palmer's trial testimony focused on the plot and the events leading up to the murder. The main conflict between the prosecution and the defense was not in the actual events or the content of the discussions that took place between Palmer and Rowell, but on the origins of these conversations. The prosecution held that Palmer only led the exchanges for the first four days after the initial comment made in late August. It was the prosecution's contention that after that period the dialog was started and controlled by Rowell. The origin of the plan was important to the prosecution since it placed more of the responsibility on Rowell rather than Palmer.

On the stand, Palmer was asked about Jennie Rowell's supposed intimate conversations with him that had been quoted in the newspapers. Palmer went on to state that on one occasion she told him that with the exception of Lynch she had never been more intimate with any man than she was with him (Palmer). Palmer tried to explain that this was a serio-comic comment made by Jennie. This remark, however, raised the question of the level of intimacy that had existed between Palmer and Jennie. Palmer was forced to admit

that he and Mrs. Rowell had had some physical contact.

"And you kissed her?" asked the defense attorney on cross-examination.

"I did," admitted Palmer reluctantly.

It appeared the defense was offering an olive branch when they went on, "But you were along way from committing adultery with her, were you not?"

"Yes, I did not commit any crime," Palmer responded grabbing at the branch.

"Well we are not talking about a crime," the defense attorney reminded Palmer. "Unfortunately, adultery is not a crime." Pulling back the olive branch.

The defense continued to question the level of intimacy Lynch had enjoyed, asking. "Is it not true that one might go farther than you (Palmer) and still not commit adultery?"

THE GENESEE COUNTY COURTHOUSE
AS IT LOOKED AT THE TIME ROWELL WAS TRIED
COURTESY GENESEE COUNTY HISTORIAN

"Oh yes," responded Palmer, distancing himself from the perception of physical intimacy with Jennie.

In an effort to clarify a negative picture that existed after his testimony Palmer made himself very visible and was willing to talk to any reporter. Palmer considered himself much maligned by the reports of his testimony carried in virtually all the newspapers. He felt he was only guilty of trying to help a life-long friend. For his effort he had wound up the "obloquy." He consistently told the reporters he would bear any accusations in the hope his friend would be found not guilty.

Palmer also took great lengths to explain his embraces of Jennie Rowell. He wanted the people to know that they "were not actuated by any base motives," but rather they were the type of actions commonly shared among families who are close. He said that each embrace had been in either the company of Newt Rowell or his own wife or both. Further, these embraces were done "without marring the tranquility of either home." His description of her "as playful as a kitten," might have gone over had he not added, "I often engaged in a romp with her in the presence of her husband and my own wife." This line probably did little to put his feelings for Jennie in a more positive light.

The Utica newspapers were less favorable to Palmer. When the case first broke it was called the Rowell/Lynch Tragedy. After Palmer's testimony was concluded it became know as the Palmer/Rowell/Lynch Tragedy. Not only was his name added, it became the first name in the series. Palmer was also attacked as a libertine himself. *The Utica Press* reported, "He sees no harm in taking someone else's wife on his lap and would not object if any man wanted to do a similar favor for his better half." This might have been quite a treat for the lucky man who was the recipient of this trade as Mrs. Palmer, with her dark brown hair and eyes, was considered by some reporters to be the most attractive woman in Batavia. One reporter went so far as to say she had "lips like a cherry."

Perhaps a quick excerpt that appeared in *The Batavia News* entitled "Some Points for Witnesses" best illustrates Palmer's relationship with the press.

Mr. Palmer, after reading all the papers, says that a good witness should possess several important qualifications.

First-He must tell the truth.

Second – He must give testimony favorable and satisfactory to both sides at the same time.

Third – He must vindicate himself.

Fourth – He must use language that reporters cannot misconstrue.

Fifth – He must please the spectators.

During the trial Rowell was a man to study. While in the courtroom he would spend much of the time looking up at the painting on the ceiling of the courtroom. There, as a reminder to all present of the importance of the room, was the image of Lady Justice balancing the scales. He would come and go in quiet, moving like a shadow not a force. Other men were touched by his problems. Often one of the other men present would shake his hand as if a gentle grasp would assure Newt of their support.

The Defense

As soon as the prosecution rested the defense made a motion that the judge instruct the

ACTUAL COURTROOM WHERE ROWELL WAS TRIED
COURTESY GENESEE COUNTY HISTORIAN

jury to render a verdict of not guilty thus throwing out the case. The defense's argument was simple. In their opinion even the testimony of the prosecution's witness had recognized that Rowell was stressed, anxious and wrought over his wife's behavior. Of course he was not sane at the moment he fired the shot, therefore, he must be acquitted on the basis of insanity.

It took the judge no time to deny the request and tell the defense to proceed with the case. Denied the instant insanity verdict the defense attorney began a speech that not only outlined their position but so maligned the members of the prosecution team for even bringing forth such a case that a loud applause was heard at points during Watson's opening statement.

There were three people who had sat at the prosecution's table each day. One was District Attorney North who had led the case and examined each of the witnesses. North had also been in the case before the grand jury. Judge Bangs of Buffalo, a man described as "shrewd and calculating" joined North. It was the third man who truly roused the emotions of the crowd. That man was John E. Brandegee of Utica (the Brandegee name was spelled differently in the various newspapers). Brandegee was a close personal friend of Johnson Lynch. It was rumored that he had volunteered to help the prosecution. The very presence of an "outsider" at the table created a breach the defense plowed through. In their opening the defense cried out before the courtroom that this man was "an emissary of revenge and a representative of a society, which promotes adultery and protects adulterers." One can only imagine the emotions that had to rush through the lawyers as they heard the outcry and applause from those in attendance. The defense must have felt a rush of unbridled encouragement. The prosecution must have understood that they had virtually no community support.

When order was finally restored the judge told the court that one more outburst like that would cause him to have the room cleared and those who led the disturbance would be arrested.

The defense went on to portray Lynch in the most unfavorable light. The lawyers told how he had an ancestry traceable back as far as the Mayflower with a forefather who was the second president of the United States. They pointed out how he wasted his heritage hanging around his uncle's law office (Arthur B. Johnson). The implication was that Lynch was not really a lawyer merely someone who was accepted to practice before the bar. Showing his drive for undeserved indulgence the defense pointed out that Lynch traveled without money, ate at his father's table and worst of all "gratified his lust in the beds of other men." To a jury of struggling farmers who worked fourteen hours a day and even then were never caught up on their work and were always trying to figure out how to pay their bills, this was a man to despise.

After a lunch break, the defense was less abusive to Brandegee. The lawyer for the defense said he wasn't really sure why Brandegee was in the court but hoped his motivations were good. The tone of this part of the defense attorney's presentation was low and without inspiration. The semi-apology had to have a little effect on the jury that had hours before heard a round of applause when the same man was attacked.

The defense ended its opening arguments with a more straightforward position. It was the case in Victorian society that a husband held a property interest in his wife. Lynch's intimacy with Jennie Rowell was no different under these rules than if he had ransacked the bureau of Rowell's private rooms, removing the most valuable treasures. In the Rowell household Jennie was a jewel defiled by Lynch.

If that property argument failed to win the necessary support of the jury, the first backup was justifiable homicide. The basis of this defense was Lynch's size and the fact that as he left the bed Lynch appeared ready to attack Rowell. The defense held throughout the trial that Rowell had shot for fear that Lynch was about to attack him.

The third line of defense was the relatively new and still undefined issue of temporary insanity. The focus of this argument was based on an origin both in genetic insanity and the stress brought on by his wife's infidelity. During the course of the trial numerous members of Rowell's family were called on to testify to the insanity of other members of the family. If each witness was telling the truth, this is one gene pool that should have been forever closed due to uncontrolled contamination.

The defense hammered on the point of Palmer being more than a mere catalyst, holding that he was more appropriately described as the feeder of the fuel that was constantly heating up the brew. At the very least, the defense tried to paint Palmer as the match that ignited the flames of jealousy, hatred and revenge. The defense tried to lay virtually all the blame in the planning on Palmer, admitting he did not actually pull the trigger but that like a professional puppeteer he had pulled Rowell's strings to such an extent that it was not even Rowell's hand that truly held the gun. To the defense the hand that held the gun was actually an extension of Palmer's desire.

Most of the witnesses for the defense were put on the stand to either testify to Rowell's good character, his mental instability after hearing of his wife's infidelity or both.

The defense attempted to place into evidence three of the letters found on Lynch's body. The letters in question were all from married women. The prosecution objected saying that they were not related to any person in the case. The defense argued that they would show that Johnson Lynch was a professional libertine who preyed on the affections of married women. The defense lawyers argued that Lynch's behavior toward the sanctity of marriage paralleled that of a professional burglar toward a person's property. He would take what he wanted regardless of to whom it belonged. The judge sustained the prosecutor's objection and the letters were not admitted. The jury, however, had heard the defense's position.

Shortly after the defense asked for the letters found on Lynch to be placed into evidence, a Buffalo newspaper published what it claimed was the contents of one of the correspondences.

Utica Oct. 27th 1883

Dear, dear J. – Little pet, please forgive me for not writing before, but he is home all the time and watches me like a mouse, but I will steal a march on him as soon as I can, you bet.

The other day when your note came he was sitting in the room and I was so "fraid" that he would see me that I did not know what to do, but it turned out all right. Now, pet, if you want to rite, [sic] send it to the office address ____, and answer this one by the same post office.

Good bye, pet, until I can see you again; it will all blow over in a little while.

Yours,

The defense had also used a highly emotional defense and an unofficial emotional appeal. They had Julia Rowell, Newt's sister, bring his two beautiful daughters to court each day. To be sure they had the maximum impact, she would usually come into the room a little after the days session had begun. Then as the jury watched she would take off the girls' bonnets, exposing their beautiful blond hair. To keep the girls occupied and behaving well she would read to them. The impact of the two polite girls and their responsible aunt – without their immoral mother – was a powerful picture. One that was never spoken by the defense attorneys but one they always kept in front of the jury members.

***

Two unnamed witnesses were brought in to town from Utica but did not actually take the stand. These two men both said to reporters that they had warned Lynch about his preoccupation with having relations with married women. These men felt that there was a very real possibility that Lynch could be shot by an irate husband. According to the accounts in the newspapers Lynch had responded to each, "Only one husband in ten shoots, and he never hits anything."

***

Expert witnesses were a relatively new concept in criminal trials. Since the case was so straightforward, expert witnesses presented the most interesting testimony. In this case the experts were the physicians who were specializing in the treatment of the insane. When asked by the defense if a sane person would take a series of actions (all actions credited to Rowell) they would answer no. Upon cross-examination by the prosecution and given a slightly different set of circumstances they would rule the same person sane. The physicians' testimony seemed to drive the jury crazy as some of the questions were over a hundred words long.

At the time of the trial epileptic seizures were considered precursors of insanity. Witness said that on at least one occasion Newt Rowell had had a seizure. One of his seizures was as an adult. During the trial Newt's sister, Julia Rowell, had a seizure in the courtroom. Following her attack in the courtroom her condition was reported daily in the newspapers.

***

The ultimate question was whether the jury would act according to law or emotion. The facts in this case were undisputed. Rowell had shot Lynch. The question became, was it an act of passion, thus he would be guilty, or self-defense because the smaller Rowell feared the much larger Lynch? There was also the loosely argued defense of insanity. The feelings of virtually the entire community were that Rowell had every right to shoot Lynch. The problem for the prosecution and the hope of the defense was that the feelings of the community, that Rowell was justified in his action, would be present among the jurors.

***

Judge Haight had just finished charging the jury when Defense Attorney Sutton asked the judge to modify his charge by instructing the jury that if after the first shot Rowell saw Lynch rising and then fired in self-defense they should bring in a ruling of "not guilty." Sutton also asked that the judge clarify that if, because of darkness, Rowell felt he was being attacked then the jury should hold that it was self-defense. Judge Haight modi-

fied his charge to include each of the changes Sutton suggested. At 5:25 in the afternoon the judge ended his charge and the deliberations began. The judge required the jurors to meet that evening for a while after they had dinner but told them that if they did not reach a verdict by 10:00 they should recess until the next day.

The jury had been sequestered in one of the hotels for the entire trial. Since the trial ended each day at 5:30 they had their evenings off. They had gotten in the habit of attending plays and musicals each evening. One newspaper went so far as to wonder, in an editorial, how these farmers were going to go back to their fields and barns after such an exciting period in their lives.

When the judge finished the jury went to their hotel for dinner. Rowell accepted a dinner offer to share the evening meal with the sheriff and his family. Most of those in attendance felt a verdict of not guilty would come in late that evening. A few were sure that the jury would not be able to reach a decision. Not a single voice was heard from the spectators at the trial that deemed a guilty verdict was a possibility.

At 6:40 the jury had finished dinner and accepted mints as they climbed the stairs of the hotel to begin their deliberations. The next day the newspapers carried reports of what had happened in the discussions. One unnamed juror took over immediately; calling for everyone who felt Rowell should be found not guilty to go to

SITE OF THE VICTORY CELEBRATION
THE WASHBURN HOUSE
MAINSTREET BATAVIA
COURTESY OF GENESEE COUNTY HISTORIAN

one wall and those who were for guilty to go to the opposite wall. All twelve men went to the not guilty wall. Before they could call for the judge one of the jurors reminded his peers that they had been asked if they found Rowell not guilty then they had to determine if it was on the basis of insanity or self-defense. The first juror said all for self-defense go to the opposite wall and all for insanity stay where they were. All twelve men walked across the room. In less than two minutes Rowell had been found not guilty on the basis that his actions were in self-defense.

Everyone was stunned when the town's bell rang so quickly, signaling that a verdict had been reached. It took fifteen minutes for everyone involved in the case to be gathered in the court-room. Rowell and the sheriff were the last two to enter the packed courtroom.

When the verdict was read aloud Rowell's head dropped to his chest, tears of joy visible on his cheeks. This time the judge could not stop the roar of the crowd. Few heard the judge order that Rowell be released immediately. The crowd of well-wishers pushed forward each trying to grasp Rowell's hand.

Eventually Rowell and his brother led the throng into the street and eventually on to the Washburn House. In the lower floor the crowd continued to shout until they were hoarse. Rowell and some of his closest associates sequestered themselves in a room on the second floor. Eventually, the landlord prevailed upon Rowell to go down and say a few words to his supporters so the crowd could leave.

Rowell did as asked, stopping on the first step to speak. By standing on the first step Rowell was barely taller than those in the crowd. After a few words of thanks the crowd formed a line with each man wanting to shake Rowell's hand.

After about ten minutes Rowell went back upstairs. He escaped his supporters by climbing out a second story window and climbing down a ladder that had been provided. He and his broth-er used back streets to get back to his family in his home on Bank Street. There, those he really cared for embraced him.

PICTURE OF E. NEWT ROWELL
APPROXIMATELY 1903
COURTESY OF HOLLAND PATTON MUSEUM

One reporter broke from the crowd and went to interview Jennie Rowell. This was the same *News* reporter whom she had granted an interview to clear up the article in the *Times*. The reporter wanted to get Jennie's feelings about the verdict. Standing in the middle of the room a newspaper in hand Jennie assured the reporter, "I am glad. I wouldn't want him to go to jail for what I have done." Jennie's mother echoed her thoughts.

The throng in the Washburn House spilled out into the street. They went into alleys and pulled out old barrels and other wooden objects with which to start a bonfire. The victory frolic in the street continued for an hour and a half until a heavy lake effect winter storm drove the crowd home to the warmth of their own hearths.

Over the next several days virtually every

newspaper had an editorial on the verdict. Most of the loud voices supported the jury's decision. Some newspapers in more of a whisper suggested that the jury had ignored the law. They didn't like the idea that Rowell should go to prison but rather that the jury should have convicted him and the governor should have pardoned him the next day.

In the editorials that followed, there was a renewed call for adultery being classified as a felony punishable by time in jail. This call went nowhere as many of the legislators would have had to make reservations in the jails for themselves.

In the months that followed, Rowell went back to work as a salesman for Palmer. During the spring and summer reporters interviewed Rowell several times. Each time he assured the reporter that he was getting his life back together. In August he visited Jennie almost by accident. Based on their meeting rumors abounded that a reconciliation was brewing. This proved not to be true as they were divorced.

Epilogue

In a period when many people, who had an incident in their past, moved west in an effort to redefine themselves, Newt Rowell never left his new home in Batavia. Shortly after the trial Rowell started his own paper box factory in Batavia. The business was successful and was incorporated in 1885 as E. N. Rowell Inc. He proved to be a successful inventor as well as a profitable businessman. At the time of his death Rowell held several patents on equipment important to the processes related to the manufacture of paper boxes.

In 1915, Rowell married for a second time. His second wife was approximately the same age as his daughters. He built his second wife the beautiful home at the corner Elliott and Park, across from the New York State School for the

THE ROWELL MANSION IN BATAVIA
THIS HOME WAS BUILT FOR HIS SECOND WIFE MARY OR "MAY"
THIS BEAUTIFUL HOME STANDS AT THE CORNER OF ELLIOT AND RICHMOND

Blind. He lived for another fourteen years dying in December 1929. His second wife continued to operate the business. The business finally closed in the late 1960s.

Johnson Lynch's parents, John Stoughton Lynch and Sarah Adams Lynch, had five children. The surviving son, James DePeyster Lynch, was born in 1868 and died in 1918, six weeks before his fiftieth birthday. James had a family of his own. There were three daughters in the older Lynch's family: Abigail Louisa, born 1850, died 1932; Anne born 1858 and G. Gertrude born 1861. None of the three daughters of the Lynchs ever married. Lynch's mother, Sarah, founded the Ladies Aid Society and the three daughters were active members. For fifty years the society met in the Lynch's Plant Street home. The mother, Sarah, died in 1907, on October 30, the anniversary of her son, Johnson Lynch's, death. Anne and Gertrude lived together their entire lives. On March 21, 1942,- both sisters died. Gertrude died of natural causes a few minutes after midnight; Anne was not told of her sister's death but died at 3:30 p.m., also of natural causes. They were together in life and are at rest next to each other in the family plot. Although there were two nephews born to brother James, the two sisters were considered, at least by one of the local newspapers, to be the last members of this prominent family.

In some inexplicable way the outcomes of E. Newton Rowell and Johnson Lynch, which clashed so violently in late October 1882, became reversed. Lynch was born to a great family. He had every potential for success – looks, intelligence, and he was charming. Yet he died before his time the result of a life of infamy. And there is little besides a stone to show that he ever lived. Rowell who was a quiet introspective man had successes that are visible even today. At one point Rowell employed more than 400 people.

The tremendous political base that was established in Utica had already started to erode at the time of the shooting. The height of the power was probably in 1868 when Conkling was a senator and Seymour ran for president. At the very least the power base in Utica was on the decline with Conkling's resignation from his senate seat in 1880.

During the course of doing the research on this case, the suicides of three single women, who were from either Utica or Rome were discovered. All three suicides were during the four months that this case took from the shooting until the trial and editorials were over. One of the women was the daughter of a former mayor of Utica. When this young woman learned that her former lover was marrying someone else in New York City, she took a train to the city. When she got to the room where her former lover was enjoying his honeymoon she pulled a gun and in front of the recently joined couple shot herself dead. This probably spoiled the honeymoon and put a damper on the marriage. The other two suicides were less dramatic but just as violent. Each was the result of the young single woman succumbing to the physical wishes of the man she assumed she would marry.

Too often we look back on the Victorian era as if it held some form of mystical morality. Too the extent this period held individuals to a higher moral standard, and that is very doubtful, it led to an equally low in acceptance of people who had made even one mistake. There is little evidence that the society believed in the biblical truth of he who cast the first stone. Victorian Society, for whatever good its perceived high morals served bore too high a cost for too many who for moments failed to attain this standard.

This case leaves us with two very different considerations of the role of both men and women in Victorian society. There were two women, Jennie Rowell and Lena Bender, who were from modest means. One attached herself to a man of power to affect change; while the other attached herself to a man full of life and himself so that she might be changed. At the same time we have two men, Johnson Lynch, a man born to everything we aspire for our children who was wasting his life in the pursuit of pleasure. While of much simpler means, Rowell, was struggling to make the most of the assets he had. It is no wonder that this case epitomizes Victorian Rules.

One of the most intriguing parts of the research on this story is why no picture of Jennie could be found. *The National Police Gazette* published the four engravings that are included, but elected not to run one of Jennie as a courtesy for her grief. *The Batavia News* published a picture for the first three days of the trial. *The News* had the same engravings of Rowell and Lynch as the *Police Gazette*. *The News* on the third day of the trial published an engraving of Jennie. This engraving was totally colored out by someone, and is only a black smear on the microfilm. One has to wonder which of the five people obliterated the picture. The only logical options are: Newt, Newt's second wife, his two daughters or Jennie. Based on the fact that the pictures of the two men remain intact, it is logical to assume that the person who did it was either Rowell's second wife or more likely Jennie.

There is one more very troubling part of this case. We have a man who out of love for his wife kills her lover. Then he never lives with her again. To love someone so much that you would kill out of jealousy yet not be able to forgive is a perplexing trait. This behavior will be seen again in a story, currently in the research stages, where a Civil War general returns home and shoots a state assemblyman. In that story we have three US senators involved.

Visiting the Sites Today

Even a hundred and twenty-five years after the crime Utica and Batavia provide some excellent venues to visit for those who like to experience the scene of the crime. There is a sense of history in each of the communities that has allowed much of the communities' historical

IN THE YEARS BETWEEN HIS TWO MARRIAGES ROWELL LIVED FOR SOME TIME IN THE RICHMOND HOTEL
THE HOTEL WAS OWNED BY W. C. WATSON HIS DEFENSE ATTORNEY
COURTESY OF HOLLAND PATTON MUSEUM

THE OLDER OF E. N. ROWELL'S FACTORIES FROM WHICH HE CONTINUED THE PRODUCTION OF PAPER BOXES
COURTESY OF HOLLAND PATTON MUSEUM

THE NEWER OF E. N. ROWELL'S FACTORIES
THIS BUILDING STOOD DIRECTLY ACROSS FROM THE COURTHOUSE WHERE ROWELL WAS TRIED
COURTESY HOLLAND PATTON MUSEUM

buildings to remain intact.

Batavia

When Johnson Lynch arrived in Batavia on the night of the shooting he had trouble finding the Rowells' new home. There were two reasons for his trouble. One problem was that it would have been dark when he got into a town he did not know. Second, Batavia has the unique trait of naming streets with two different names as one crosses a main street.

For additional support or information about Batavia visit the Richmond Library, the Holland Patton Office Museum on Main Street and the historian's office also on Main Street.

The Courthouse

The old courthouse on Main Street has been converted into an office building used by the county. This is actually advantageous since the courtroom where Rowell was tried is now the meeting room of the Genesee County Legislature. What a pleasure it is to see this one grand room where so much has happened still in its original condition. For once a space was not cut up into minimal size workspaces.

When one enters this grand old edifice from the park side it is easy to imagine Rowell and his attorneys climbing the stairs on their way to a day in front of the jury. Inside the building, at the top of the circular stairways, the large wood doors give the impression of substance. This building is one of the best examples of the righteousness that the law and lawyers had in the 1870s. Credit should be given to those who, when the building was being updated, took care that the integrity of the building was maintained.

The Rowell Factories

The factories that Rowell owned are now gone, the victims of urban renewal. His largest and most recent plant stood at the site of the new county courthouse in Batavia. There are pictures at the historian's office, which is next door to the courthouse, that show the Rowell factory as a backdrop to the county courthouse. One has to wonder what thoughts went through Rowell's mind when he looked out the window of his factory and looked on the scene of his trial.

The Scene of the Shooting

Of all the crimes that have been reported in the various books published by Deep Roots Publications this is the only crime scene that is in virtually the same state as it was at the time of the incident.

The house at 123 Bank Street is still a private residence and people trying to get a sense for the scene should be respected. The house is small-

E. NEWT ROWELL WITH HIS SECOND WIFE MAY
IN THE OFFICE OF THEIR FACTORY
COURTESY OF HOLLAND PATTON MUSEUM

er than one might have assumed, since Rowell was the owner of a manufacturing business. The main reason for the size is that, at the time the house was contracted, Rowell was just starting out as an entrepreneur. Add to his limited wealth the facet that the Rowell family had been living in a hotel for over a year, it is obvious that even this size home must have seemed spacious.

Standing on the street it is possible to see the porch from which Rowell called to his neighbor for help. It is obvious from the placement of the window to see that the stairway is on the north side of the house.

William Palmer lived on Washington

LYNCH'S STONE IN OAKWOOD CEMETARY UTICA
NOTE: IT IS LEANING FORWARD

THE MONUMENT TO ROWELL
GRAND VIEW CEMETARY BATAVIA

Avenue, less than a block from the Rowells. The Palmer house has since been taken down with the area becoming a parking lot.

Rowell's Mansion

When Newt Rowell remarried in 1915, it is reported that he built the mansion at the corner of Elliott and Park as a wedding present for his new wife. This house reflects the wealth that Rowell had amassed during his life. His second wife stayed in the house until her death in the 1963.

The Grave Markers

The way individuals have their life reflected by their grave marker has always been a fascination to me. The markers for Rowell and Lynch are excellent examples of the differences that exist. Lynch's stone is in the family plot at Oak Wood Cemetery in Utica. The stones of the five siblings are all the same size. Lynch's provides the exact dates of his life. What is truly remarkable is that his stone is the only one in the plot that is leaning. In sharp contrast is Rowell's marker. The marker to his life is impressive, dramatic and yet simple. He was interred in Grand View Cemetery, just outside Batavia on Route 33 east. The cemetery is divided into clearly designated sections. Rowell is in the Highland section. If you drive around looking at the stones you will not see his name. His marker is very unusual, consisting of four marble columns supporting a lintel. His name, with no dates, is engraved across the marble stone that is supported by the columns. The stones are respectful yet strong and defining.

Utica

At the risk of offending people from Utica, it is in many ways like going back in time. Most of the old downtown is still standing and in use. You can get the feeling that if you were to replace the cars with older vehicles you could be in the 1920s.

Lynch Family Home

The Lynch family lived in the row of homes on Plant Street referred to as the Comstock Block. These are early examples of brownstones that would fit perfectly into the homes of London.

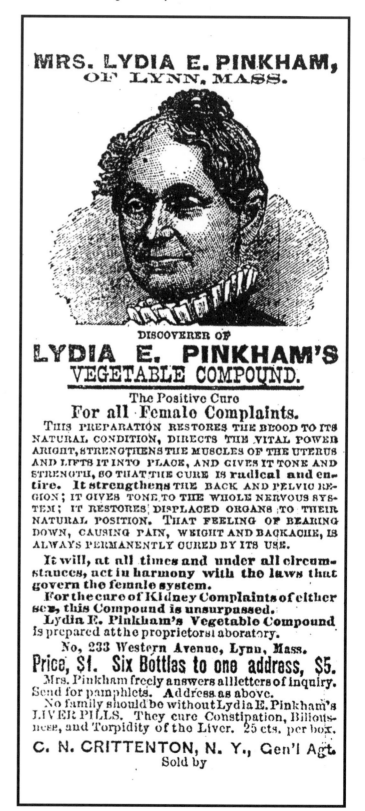

Galway

Arms on the Street

On Monday and Tuesday, January 24th and 25th, 1876, the various newspapers in the region were reporting that all the men of the area around Galway were carrying a sidearm, shotgun or a rifle. In the case of some men they were carrying more than one weapon. As the residents of Galway walked through the streets, of what they had always previously considered to be a quiet hamlet, they were constantly looking over their shoulders for a possible assailant. The fear among the inhabitants was so intense that women did not walk the streets unescorted. Children, if they were even allowed outside, played only in their own yard or, if bold, in their immediate neighborhoods. For those two days it was as if a dark cloud of fear had suddenly adopted the community. Throughout the village and surrounding farms both of those long winter nights there was a silent foreboding.

A Body Found

In this incident, the anxiety within the hamlet was not unfounded paranoia. On Sunday morning, as their neighbor Consider Case drove his family to church, he found an unconscious man on the icy embankment next to the wagon track. The man was barely alive having survived what, based on the marks on his face, appeared to be a severe beating and a night in the extreme elements of a cold January. The combined effects of the excessively cold night and the battering to the forehead had left the man gravely disfigured and his skin frozen. Taking the man into Galway, it took a while before someone was able to identify the man as one they had seen the day before get off the stage, claiming he was a relative of Jacob Fonda. Fonda resided on Foster Hill. When Case took the man to Fonda's house it took Jacob several minutes to recognize him as his 45-year-old cousin, Sanford Fonda of Sharon Springs, Schoharie County.

After dropping the battered man at Fonda's home, the Case family continued on their way to their church services. Having been involved in one of the region's biggest events in many years and having committed the unspeakable act of being late for church, when the services ended the Cases felt compelled to spread the news of their morning discovery.

Like all other Sundays in the days before radio and television, when the worship ended most of the community gathered and visited around the church. The social climate was perfect for reaching supposed conclusions as to the events involved in the case. After church, in a small community like Galway, everyone with knowledge of the stranger or the events of the previous evening was in one place. The magnitude of the news and the rampant gossip regarding the presumed circumstances in the story led to conclusions being quickly developed.

Disturbing Circumstances

Before anyone pulled their buggy out of the churchyard, it was understood that Sanford had arrived by the Amsterdam stagecoach late Saturday afternoon. It was learned that when he paid the stage driver he had a large roll of bills with him. Unfortunately for Sanford, he had stopped at the saloon. The bartender, a man known as Harris, poured him a glass of ale and provided him with directions to his cousin's home. Sanford Fonda left the saloon after finishing his one drink. It was immediately supposed, by those gathered that Sunday, that shortly after Sanford left the saloon, unidentified men followed him out the door. All the parishioners suspected that the robbers had seen him pay for his drink with a dollar extracted from a large roll of bills. Not one person doubted that in the secluded spot where his body had been found men bent on robbery had set upon him. There was considerable debate

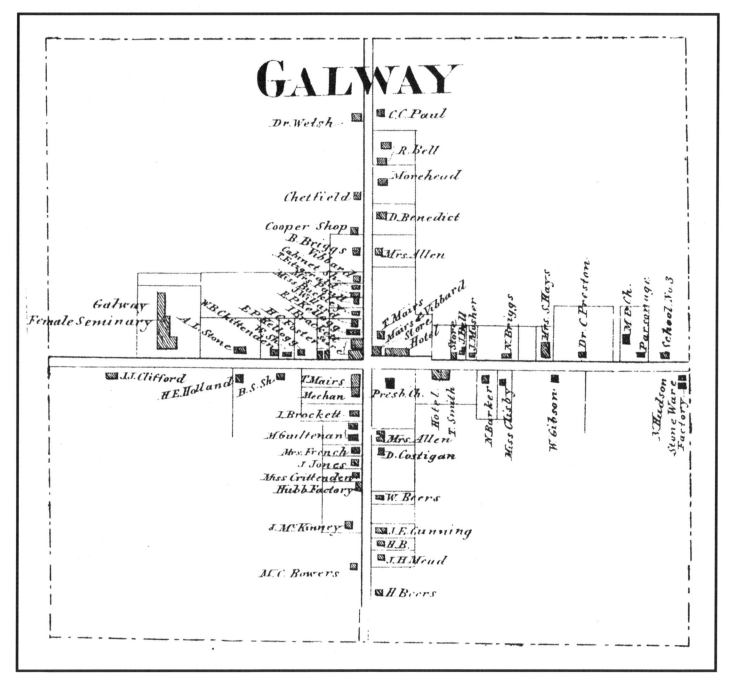

GALWAY

Dr. Welsh · C.C. Paul · R. Bell · Morehead · Chetfield · D. Benedict · Cooper Shop · B. Briggs · Mrs. Allen · Cabinet Sh. · T. Fitzgerald · Miss Buckley · B.P. Kellogg · T. Mairs · Mairs & Vibbard · Mrs. S. Hays · Dr. C. Preston · M.E. Ch. · Parsonage · School No. 3 · Galway Female Seminary · W.B. Crittenden · A.L. Stone · E.P. Kellogg · W. Sh. · B. Foster · J. Black · Store J. Bell · J. Mosher · N. Briggs · Store Hotel · J.J. Clifford · H.E. Holland · B.S. Sh. · T. Mairs · Mechan · Presb. Ch. · Hotel J. Smith · N. Barker · Miss Busby · W. Gibson · V. Hudson Stone Ware Factory · I. Brockett · M. Guiltenan · Mrs. Allen · D. Costigan · Mrs. French · J. Jones · Miss Crittenden · Hubb Factory · W. Beers · J. McKinney · J.E. Cunning · H.B. · J.H. Mead · M.C. Bowers · H. Beers

MAP FROM ATLAS OF SARATOGA COUNTY 1866

as to whether the assailants were set on murder or just robbery.

Murder or Robbery

The proof that the intent was robbery not murder was provided by what was left on the victim and what was missing. Those who had seen him that morning said that Sanford had a dark bruise on his forehead. This injury could have been the result of a blow from a club. The roll of money the stage driver had reported seeing was missing. At the time he was found Sanford only had six cents in his pocket. One of the disturbing facts was that Sanford still had his valuable gold watch and chain with him when he was discovered. Since everyone in the congregation suddenly considered themselves a master detective, the watch was rapidly explained as proof the robbers were professional. It was rationalized that a professional thief would not want to be caught with anything, like a watch, that could directly link him to the robbery. The members of the congregation reasoned that since the blow that caused

50

the head wound was not severe enough to cause immediate death it was obvious the intent was strictly robbery and not murder.

Any question as to the likelihood of a random assault was eliminated on the way home from church. When the inquisitive went to the site, they found a pair of footprints in the snow leading through a field away from the scene. It was obvious to them that for the assailants to have cut across a field, they had to have known the area and all the surrounding roads. The assailants had to be people familiar with the area. It was instantly time to take all necessary measures to protect one's family.

The Victim

Despite his injuries and the exposure, Sanford held desperately to the threads of life until 4:00 o'clock Monday morning. Unfortunately for Sanford, the night's exposure finished the job started by the robbers and removed him from the pain of being among the living and sent him to the peace of the those who have traveled the last journey alone.

Not knowing who among them had taken a person's life, it was only natural that all the men were carrying firearms as they worked in their barns or walked the streets.

Inquest

The county coroner, Dr. Benjamin West Noxon of Ballston Spa, arrived in Galway on Tuesday to conduct an inquest into Sanford Fonda's death. All the citizens of the hamlet of Galway hoped that the inquest would lead to the discovery of the identity of the villain(s) so that he or they could be punished for the horrible misdeed.

Coroner's Jury Called

In front of a full-capacity crowd, Coroner Noxon called six witnesses to the stand. Noxon had created a coroner's jury so he could investigate the circumstances in this action.

Consider Case was to now have his fifteen minutes of fame. He told of the discovery of the wounded man near the church in Galway. He stressed for the jury the bodily injuries on poor Fonda. Case also stressed for his neighbors the care his family had provided the poor victim.

The victim's cousin, Jacob Fonda - the man the victim had come to visit, was the next person called by the coroner. Jacob told the corner's jury of Sanford's arrival at his home. Jacob went on to tell of Sanford's subsequent suffering and death despite his family's medical support.

All is not as it Seemed

The next man to testify began to change the perception of what had happened to Sanford. Sebastian Fonda, Sanford's father, told the coroner how his son had left his employment as a clerk in Troy the previous July. Sanford had worked for a Mr. Klock for seven years but of late had developed "dissipated habits." Since the previous July, Sanford had lived with his father and other relatives. Sebastian, like any laudable father, had supplied his son with money on which to survive during his troubled times. According to Sebastian, the last money he had given Jacob was $10 at the beginning of December.

The understanding of the events took yet another turn when Sylvester Barnett, the stage driver, contradicted the stories of Sanford's great wealth that had been circulating for the previous two days. Barnett told Noxon's jury that Fonda had only shown him money enough to pay his fare and had not revealed a roll of money. Based on Barnett's testimony, a motive for robbery was now coming into question.

The next witness's testimony showed that Sanford had wanted to brace himself for the cold. Charles Curtis, who owned and operated Curtis's Hotel in Galway, reported that Sanford had not just stopped at the saloon but had also stopped at his hotel bar for a drink to ward off the elements. Curtis had sold him a glass of whiskey, which Sanford had finished just before he left. Curtis told the jury that Fonda's departure was just as it was getting dark.

On the stand the Rev. Richard Ryder told of how on Saturday evening as he was making his final preparations for Sunday's services he had been interrupted when Sanford had knocked on his door and asked that he be allowed to warm himself by the fire. As Sanford warmed his body, Rev. Ryder had confirmed the directions Sanford had been given to find his cousin Jacob's home.

As he slipped slowly from life's woes, Sanford Fonda had been treated by Dr. Von Allen. On the stand, Von Allen told the coroner that it was his belief that the bruises on the victim's forehead had been caused by a fall and were not the result of a blow from a club. He had reached this conclusion based on the shape of the bruise, which was uneven and jagged.

The inquiry and story ended with the testimony of Abraham Chesney. Chesney and his neighbor lived one road over from the scene of the assault. When they heard of the "murder" they had walked over to the site. After visiting the location the two decided that it was too cold to take the road back to their homes. The two resolved that rather than take the roads they would save time and cut across the fields. Theirs were the footprints in the snow.

After the testimony the coroner's verdict was anticipated to be exactly what it turned out. The jury determined that Sanford Fonda died as a result of "convulsions and exposure."

With the combined villains of alcohol and cold identified, the people of Galway returned their weapons to their closets and went back to their simpler lives, reminded again that all is rarely as it first appears.

The true crime in this case was not murder but rather rumor enhanced by amateur detective work and the reporting in newspapers of conclusions not facts. But then again it was the 1870s and newspapers were not subject to the same rules as today. We can all be comforted that this same type of reporting would never happen in the 21st century. Or would it?

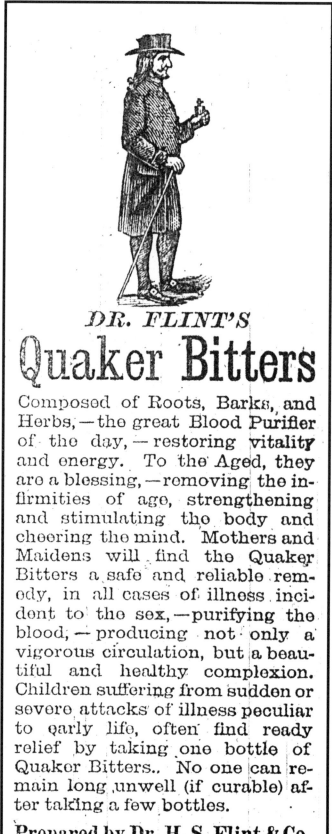

The Amazing Dr. Allen

It was a cold January night when two men, from opposite ends of the social and intellectual spectrum, worked quietly at their mission. The last thing they needed was to be heard as they carried the body of the dead woman down the stairs. To be sure, the body would not be detected, the older and poorer of the men had sat with the corpse in a locked third floor bedroom the entire day. The wea!thier man wanted to insure secrecy during the removal of the body from the house. He planned the evening so that the two men and the body would be on the stairs as the other residents were having their evening tea. The last thing the ambitious younger man needed now was to be detected by one the numerous other occupants of the house. Without setting the body down, the two men took it out of what was considered the main house and placed it on a bench in an attached area, referred to commonly as the cottage. While the poorer man waited with the deceased, the owner of the house went across Lafayette Street to the stable where he hitched his horse to his cutter. When the sleigh was pulled up to the cottage door the two men lifted the cloak-clad body into the open backspace on the cutter. The lifeless form lay in the area usually reserved for baggage. Without uttering a word the two men drove the five short blocks to the cemetery.

Minutes after it left the house the cutter arrived at the southeast corner of Green Ridge Cemetery. The section they were in was along the fence in the extreme back, in an area of the cemetery reserved for those who could not afford a burial plot. It was known as potter's field. There the men found an open grave dug exactly where it had been contracted. Beside the grave was a plain hemlock box with the lid open. They had expected a pine casket but by this time and under these circumstances they had to accept the cheap substitute. The men were, after all, hardly in a position to ask for either their money back or demand the casket that they had paid for. After placing the body in the inferior box the two men lowered their encumbrance into the dark, cold grave. The owner of the cutter knew that he would be missed if he did not get back to the big house, so he threw a few shovels of dirt into the dark cavity then told his confederate to finish filling the grave.

The man who was left behind was in no frame of mind to handle the situation. He had spent the whole day locked in a room with the dead woman. To add to the stress of his emotional burden, the body he had sat with had belonged to his wife. The pressure was too much for this poor, simple individual. He was suddenly so saddened by what had happened and by what he perceived as the ill treatment of his wife's body, that he became, in his own words, "much broken up." He went to his own home, leaving the hole, and the secrets it was supposed to protect, open for the night.

***

There are crimes, which may appear relatively innocuous, yet the ramifications are far deeper than anyone would anticipate. That is the case in the charges of failing to report a contagious illness that were filed against Dr. Thomas Allen of Saratoga Springs. Dr. Allen was the man that drove the cutter home so he would be in time for tea.

***

On December 23, 1875, Dr. Allen had left his practice in Saratoga Springs to visit friends and family in Canada. Although in practice for nine years, Dr. Allen lived and practiced in a new brick boarding house he owned on the corner of Circular and Lafayette Streets in Saratoga Springs. By today's standards the house was enormous. It had been built to rent out rooms to boarders. Boarding houses of the Victorian times were like apartment complexes today with a large range in the quality and security. In Dr. Allen's house many of the boarders were relatively successful and all were respectable. Among his boarders were

MEDICAL INSTITUTE, T. E. ALLEN, M. D.
CORNER OF CIRCULAR AND LAFAYETTE STREET
COURTESY OF SARATOGA SPRINGS PUBLIC LIBRARY

a minister, a teacher, an architect, and several people engaged in sales. At the time of his trip there were fourteen boarders residing in the house. Dr. Allen was an ambitious man, convinced that he was practicing the form of medicine that would shape the future. It was his plan to convert the boarding house in which he lived into a medical institute. There was, at the time, the Stone Institute also on Circular Street in Saratoga. Dr. Stone's institute was between Phila and Spring Street. Stone's institute treated those who had protracted illness, while also providing housing for their families. Dr. Allen's would also be a college. In his mind, Dr. Allen's institute would be the ultimate tribute to the success brought on by his skills and the form of treatment that he was convinced would ultimately change medicine forever.

While on his Canadian excursion Dr. Allen

left his younger brother, Asa, in charge of the boarding house. Asa was scheduled to graduate from a medical school in New York City in early February so unofficially he also took charge of his brother's medical practice.

In the tradition of the day, the room rate at boarding houses included meals. In October 1875, Dr. Allen had hired Mrs. Ella Lewis to cook the meals for his tenants. Ella, her husband, and her two children lived in an apartment over the carriage house of one of the mansions on South Broadway. Her husband, Job Lewis, claimed to be a butler in the grand hotels of Saratoga during the season; however, it is more likely he was, at most, a waiter and more likely a busboy. In the 1870s the season in Saratoga was the entire summer.

Exactly what happened to poor Ella will never be clear. What we do know is that young Carrie Chase who resided in a boarding house on

DR. ALLEN MEDICAL INSTITUTE
EXACTLY IN THE CENTER OF THE PICTURE
PUBLISHED AND DRAWN BY L. R. BURLEIGH, TROY, N. Y. 1884

Washington Street had recently visited Syracuse. Soon after she left that city there was an outbreak of smallpox. Carrie showed no signs of the illness until after she was back in Saratoga. Exactly when Ella and Carrie were in contact with each other is not certain, what is known is that Dr. Allen successfully treated Carrie. It is possible that the doctor carried the germs in the heavy coat that he wore that winter.

Two different stories regarding what transpired in the medical treatment of Ella were reported. Ella's husband, Job, told one of the stories. Dr. Thomas Allen and several of the other residents of the boarding house told a similar story that was significantly different on key points.

In addition to the question of what happened to Ella is the matter of the motivation of those who sought to prosecute Dr. Allen. The practice of medicine was in transition in the 1870s. This transition was brought on in part because during the Civil War when soldiers went to the hospital it was often the equivalent of admitting the inevitability of their own death. Germs spread in the makeshift hospitals and men with minor wounds too often died of infections. The category of medicine practiced by Dr. Allen was very different from that practiced by the doctors who would testify against him. Dr. Allen was trained as a homoeopathist. Homeopathic treatments were one of the new forms of medicine that were being explored during this time period. Homeopathic doctors were relatively new and were a result of a school where doctors treated like with like. Dr. Allen's training led him to believe that drugs that caused a reaction within the body similar to that caused by the disease being treated should be used as a remedy for an illness. In addition to homeopaths, there were doctors who trained to be hydropaths, using the cures of water, and eclectics, those who used botanical treatments. Traditional medicine (allopathic) held that medicines should be used that counteracted the symptoms. All the doctors who came out against Dr. Allen were allopathically trained. They believed that it was appropriate to treat an illness with drugs that caused the opposite reaction to the illness, not those that resembled it. Regardless of the form of medicine practiced there was one common thread that is gone from today's practices. The doctor went to the home. The patient did not go to the doctor. By the year 1915 allopathic physicians had won the contest becoming the predominate form of medicine.

In all probability there was an underlying force that affected both the traditionally trained physicians of the city and the young impertinent, Dr. Allen. Dr. Allen's plan of turning his boarding house into a medical institute would have been in direct opposition to the allopathic doctors' training and beliefs. After all, if Dr. Allen's institute were successful it would further the theories of homeopathic medicine. Since before the Revolutionary War, people had been coming to Saratoga Springs to seek the healing effects of the various mineral spring waters. Dr. Allen's institute may have made Saratoga Springs, a city already recognized as a center for natural cures of mineral water, the center for homeopathic medicine. Although they would claim it was not true, the prospect of Saratoga being a homeopathic center would have been repulsive to the traditionally taught physicians. To be involved in a medical scandal where patients were dying would have been equally repulsive to the ambitious Dr. Allen.

On Monday afternoon, December 27th, Dr. Thomas Allen was still away. Already sick for a couple of days by that afternoon Ella Lewis began to feel very ill. Luckily for Ella, Miss Alice Burt, a teacher at the Beekman Street School and a boarder at the house, liked to bake and often worked alongside Ella in the kitchen. In the early afternoon, Ella was feeling so badly that she asked Miss Burt to get Asa. Asa visited with Ella while she was cooking dinner in the kitchen of the boarding house.

According to Asa, Ella complained of having severe abdominal and head pain. She told the "almost doctor" that her illness was "brought on by a cold." Ella at thirty-five had a three-year history of having painful menstruation. Knowing Ella's history, Asa, the "not yet" graduate, prescribed some pain relievers to be taken immediately and left Ella working at the stove. The medications that Asa prescribed were the same used to treat several diseases including a cold, flu and smallpox. Asa went so far as to suggest to Ella that she could go to bed if she felt it would help.

Later in the afternoon Asa went to check on Ella's health. Not finding her in the kitchen he went to a third-floor bedroom of his brother's boarding house where he found her resting. Asa's feeling was that Ella had not improved since he saw her in the early afternoon, so he prescribed a second dose of the same medications.

Ella's husband, Job Lewis, claimed that he was sent for this day because of his wife's condition. Job said that in the message he received he was told that she was very weak. Job went on to say that even this, the first day that Ella was ill enough to request a doctor; she was "distracted" by the severe pain.

In direct contradiction to Job's story, Asa claimed that he never sent for him to stay with her. How Job came to stay with his wife was only the first of many discrepancies between what Job would report and what virtually everyone else would say. This case was in the days before the telephone. Had the prosecution had a stronger belief that Job was correct in that he was sent for that day, they would have put on the stand the person who was sent to get him.

Probably the most clear indication that Job was at best confused was his absolute declaration that as soon as he arrived Asa Allen ordered the door locked and no visitors were to be permitted. Job did modify his story, saying that on one occasion the maid, the widow Mrs. Gunn, was allowed to enter the room. In contrast several of the others in the house on the days that Ella was sick said that they had visited with her and that the door was never locked. One of those that most contradicted Job was Miss Alice Burt.

Miss Burt, a resident of the boarding house for the last year, said that she saw Ella on Christmas Day and December 26th. On both occasions Ella complained to Alice that she was not feeling well but did not ask to see Asa. Even after Ella was sick enough that she elected to go into the third floor room to rest, Miss Burt visited her almost every day. Of even more significance to the validity of Job's truthfulness was Miss Burt's claim that he was not even in the boarding house until Wednesday the 29th.

Job Lewis was of limited mental ability. Some time later, when he was asked his age, he was not sure, claiming that he thought he was about forty. Pushed to be more accurate, he said he was sure he wasn't fifty yet. Job's mental capacity played heavily into the litigation, as he was the only witness for the prosecution that was actually present in the boarding house during the time Ella was sick. Everyone else in the boarding house during the outbreak, who was called to the stand, would testify on behalf of the doctor.

Asa visited Ella several times on Tuesday the 28th. Asa's first visit was at 9:00 a.m. At that time Asa thought he saw some improvement in Ella's condition from the previous day. So impressed was the "almost doctor" with Ella's improving condition on his second visit that day that by mid-afternoon he stopped the medication completely assuming she was on her way to a full recovery. In contrast to Asa's reports, Job maintained that Asa was concerned on Tuesday and continued to treat his Ella the entire day.

Dr. Allen returned to Saratoga on Tuesday the 28th. According to Asa he and his brother discussed Ella's condition that day. After reviewing her symptoms and Asa's perception that she was recovering, the brothers felt there was no need for Dr. Allen to see Ella that day. In sharp contrast, Job said that Dr. Allen took over the treatment of his wife on Tuesday, visiting with her about noon. Job's claim was not supported by anyone else involved.

In examining Job's reliability it should be noted that Job said that the only persons to come into his wife's room during the time she was sick were the Allen brothers and the widow, Mrs. Mary Gunn, who was the housekeeper of the boarding house. Job even limited Mrs. Gunn's visit by noting that she only came by on Tuesday to straighten up the room. Job was certain that no one else was in the room because he was with his wife the entire time, except when he returned home late in the evenings on both Monday and Tuesday. On those two evenings Job had returned to his home for the night to be sure his children were cared for. On those two nights he had left Ella to rest at the doctor's boarding house.

On Wednesday morning, December 29th, Asa stopped in to check on Ella before he left for the train that would take him back to New York City. Asa's opinion was that Ella was about the same as she had been the previous day. Asa wished Ella good luck and told her that his brother would be checking on her that afternoon.

Job Lewis would maintain that his wife was "crazy with pain" on Wednesday, Thursday and Friday. Miss Burt presented a very different picture of Ella. Miss Burt told of visiting Ella during the same three day time period. For these three days Ella was in the third floor room and Miss Burt was helping in the kitchen. Miss Burt's reason to visit Ella was to get recipes and to take her food. Miss Burt would confirm that Ella was not well, but would contradict the impression that the poor woman was "crazy with pain." Having taken over treatment, Dr. Allen also said that Ella was not well on these days, but he said that she was not crazy with pain. Dr Allen continued his brother's treatment for severe menstrual pain in conjunction with the flu. There was also a contradiction between the stories as Job said his wife had blotches on these three days while Dr. Allen and Miss Burt said none were present.

According to Job on Thursday, Dr. Allen told him that Ella had the varioloid form of smallpox. The doctor would say that there was no rash until Sunday morning. The varioloid form meant that the illness had been contracted from an inoculation. The varioloid from of smallpox was rarely fatal. In contrast confluent smallpox was passed from one person who had the infection to the next victim. The confluent form was the most serious and often claimed the life of its victim. The open sores that were associated with smallpox left many of its victims scared for life. This is the derivation of the expression pox marked, which was seen on wanted posters.

Job Lewis maintained that on Friday evening he went home to visit with his family. He returned to the boarding house on Circular Street that same evening to await the outcome of his wife's illness.

On Saturday night the fever had welled up inside Ella so much that it made her rise up from the bed. While Job was resting in a chair she ran from the room stumbling in the hallway. Hearing the noise, one of the other tenants, Fredrick Camp, opened his door and saw the poor woman laying on the floor with her husband standing over her. Camp, realizing that the woman was seriously ill, went to Dr. Allen's room to seek his aid. The three men, Camp, Dr. Allen and Job returned Ella to her bed. Camp, who was an architect in Saratoga, had stood immediately next to Ella. He did not notice any rash on Ella's skin and he was reasonably sure that in her condition she could not have opened the door, if in fact it had been locked. Like Miss Burt, Camp was now a witness who disagreed with the story told by Job Lewis.

On Sunday morning Dr. Allen again examined Ella. This time he noted that she had a "simple rash" on her arms and face. For the first time he suspected that she might have a disease other than the one for which he had been treating her. Dr. Allen maintained that on Sunday morning for the first time, and only as a precaution, he ordered Job to lock the door. Uncertain as to what Ella was suffering from, that afternoon Dr. Allen went to Dr. Frank Boyce's office to ask his opinion of the symptoms. Dr. Allen did not intend to report a case of smallpox at this time, as he did not believe that Ella had the disease. Just before bedtime on

Sunday Dr. Allen again examined Ella. At this time he found that the rash had spread and was covering her body. He again prescribed for her and left her with her husband. Dr. Allen would be adamant that he thought Ella was suffering from chickenpox not smallpox.

At 4:00 a.m. on Monday, January 3, 1876, Ella Lewis died. Her husband, Job, was the only person with her at the time. Hearing his wife's last breath escape from her chest Job went downstairs to Dr. Allen's room and told him that Ella had died. Job was very sad and told the doctor he had no way to pay for the funeral. The thought of the cost must have plagued Lewis as he sat in the dark listening to his wife struggle for breath. Dr. Allen supposedly told Job not to worry that he would take care of the arrangements. In exchange Dr. Allen told Job that he would have to stay with his wife's body until after dark that day. According to Job's story the doctor told him to remain in the room with his coat buttoned up and not to change clothes. This was the standard way to avoid the spread of smallpox and would be used by Dr. Allen's detractors as proof that he knew what Ella had died from. At least in part, Job ignored the doctor's orders and "was about the house" on several occasions during the day.

During the period of the onset of the fever until she died a week later, Job Lewis maintained that Ella Lewis never ate. All she had was a few glasses of water to drink to offset the loss caused by her constant perspiration. Miss Burt said that each day until Friday she brought food for Ella and the dishes were returned clean. Whether Ella ate the food or Job had eaten it instead is not clear.

The weather on Monday was typical of early winter with light snow and bitter cold. Dr. Allen drove Miss Burt to school, stopping on the way at Dr. Boyce's office. Dr. Allen told Miss Burt that his purpose in going to Boyce's office was that he was going to report Ella's case. Dr. Allen did not say to Miss Burt that it was a case of smallpox. Dr. Boyce, one of the members of the Board of Health, was not in so Dr. Allen left him a note. On the previous Saturday, Dr. Allen had passed Dr. Boyce on the road near the Presbyterian Church on Washington

Street. The two physicians reportedly nodded to each other but no words were exchanged. Dr. Boyce would imply that in seeing each other at this close quarters Dr. Allen could have asked him for help in his diagnosis then or have notified him of the outbreak of smallpox.

At about noon on Monday January 3rd, Dr. Allen contacted the sexton of the Greenridge Cemetery. The doctor's request was somewhat strange but would offer the sexton some always-needed funds. Dr. Allen asked the sexton to have a grave dug in the potter's field. At the doctor's expense a simple grave was dug through the frozen ground that afternoon. The grave was along the fence.

That same afternoon Dr. Allen visited a local undertaker and asked that a simple pine casket be delivered to the Greenridge Cemetery. Dr. Allen told the undertaker that he wanted the casket delivered that afternoon to a site near what would be an open grave. The undertaker thought the request strange and asked who had died. Dr. Allen responded that his cook had died. Over the following days, the undertaker told everyone that he had asked the doctor if the woman had died of chicken pox. The story changes as to the doctor's answer. According to the doctor, he said that he responded it was more serious than chicken pox. According to the undertaker the doctor said that the cause was chicken pox. The difference in the two statements was in the extent the doctor was the still trying to cover up for Ella's death. It should be noted the character of the undertaker. He admitted that he had billed Dr. Allen for a casket. When the doctor and Job got to the grave that night and when the undertaker knew that they would have no options they found themselves confronted with a simple and cheap wooden box.

While the tenants at Dr. Allen's were having their evening tea, the doctor and Job carried Ella's body down the stairs and put it in the cottage attached to the boarding house. There her barely clothed body lay on cold benches waiting while the doctor hitched his horse to the cutter in preparation for transporting it to the cemetery.

***

When the sexton went to the grave on the morning of January 4th, he found that only a couple of shovels full of dirt had been thrown onto the wooden casket. The sexton finished filling in the grave.

Exactly how the story that there was an outbreak of smallpox broke is not clear. How the newspapers discovered the case is even less clear. It is probable that the suspicious nature of the events of January 3rd triggered rumors. It is not every day that a doctor asks that a grave be dug and that a casket be delivered to a cemetery in the afternoon. It is very likely that those involved started telling others what they knew. By January fourth, just hours after the grave was closed, the Board of Health definitely knew.

Dr. Charles Grant, who was not on the Board of Health, was brought into the investigation. Dr. Grant would play a significant role in many criminal cases in Saratoga County, including the murder of Eliza Billings. This story is told in the book To Spend Eternity Alone. Dr. Grant was also the physician who treated former President Grant when he was in residence at his cottage in Wilton. Dr. Grant was extremely successful, as demonstrated by his grand brick home on the Corner of Walden and Woodlawn Street, that would later serve as the Elk's hall (the building is still standing).

As part of his investigation Dr. Grant interviewed the distraught widower, Job Lewis. Job would later say he was unable to remember what he told Dr. Grant because, "My wife had been so ill used I was nearly crazy." Based on what Job was able to report Dr. Grant called a meeting of the Board of Health. The Board of Health ordered that Ella's body be exhumed to see if there were evidence of smallpox. The man who had dug the grave on January 3rd and filled it in on the fourth, was called back to dig in the same place later in the day.

When they dug down to the bottom of the

grave they found a simple hemlock box with the name of the undertaker stamped on the outside. The undertaker would swear that he delivered a casket but it appeared Job was correct his wife's body was not treated with dignity. Dr. Grant noted that the box was broken and dirt was already on the body. Inside the simple wooden box were Ella's remains covered in an old dress that had risen up and only covered her upper body. After only a minute long examination, Dr. Grant was sure that her body was covered with confluent smallpox.

***

In the tradition of the day, the Board of Health ordered that Dr. Allen's boarding house be quarantined and that all the residents be kept inside under guard. They ordered the same for the boarding house on Washington Street where Carrie Chase lived. Over the course of the next few days the newspapers carried rumors of the possible spread of the disease. In securing the two boarding houses the Board of Health ordered the buildings be fumigated. The process of fumigation was complex. All clothing and linens for the bed had to be washed in carbolic acid. Carbolic acid was also used on the carpets. Wool clothing was all buried. The wallpaper had to be removed and replaced with new paper. So secure was the process that the glue used to install the new wallpaper had to be made with carbolic acid.

In fact smallpox did break out in one other place. One of Job Lewis children came down with the disease. The newspapers would say it was the result of Dr. Allen's giving Job his wife's bedding to take home. In one of the only letters written by Dr. Allen on the entire incident he said that he had not given Job any items and that if any had been taken from the house it was a result of Job's pilfering.

As people waited to see the extent of the outbreak stories began to appear regarding the condition of the tenants. The only other tenant of what had come to be called "Fort Allen" who contracted smallpox was Fannie Simmons. Fannie's case was considered mild and she recovered with no long-term effects. There were no other cases in

DEFENSE ATTORNEY
GENERAL BUTLER

Saratoga Springs, although there was a scare in Ballston Spa.

There were three charges filed against Dr. Allen. Each of the charges was for failure to report a case of smallpox to the Saratoga Board of Health as required under the health laws. The charges were for the cases contracted by Carrie Chase, the girl who had visited Syracuse; Fannie Simmons, a boarder at Dr. Allen's; and Ella Lewis. Job and Ella's daughter's case did not result in a charge as it developed after Dr. Allen was quarantined and he never treated the child.

The quarantine almost resulted in a positive situation for the village of Saratoga Springs. One of the residents of the boarding house was Reverend Wood. The reverend was a very popular minister. While he was held hostage in the house, it was learned that he was the candidate for a ministry in a much larger congregation in New England. His parishioners were temporarily comforted by the fact that he was unable to attend his final interview. The parishioners assumed that because he was not present he would be turned down for the new position. Apparently, the people of the new parish were suitably impressed with Reverend Wood that they held the position and he moved as soon as he and the rest of the detainees were released.

***

Justice was much swifter in the Victorian era. Dr. Allen's trial began in mid-March 1876, just two months after the outbreak. Dr. Allen's attorney, General J. B. Butler, attempted to have the trial postponed until the July term. Butler based his request on the unavailability of five essential witnesses. Two of these witnesses included people who were named on the indictments - Carrie Chase and Fannie Simmons. It also included three tenants in Dr. Allen's boarding house - Mary Dodge, Reverend Woods and the Reverend's wife. Affidavits were offered into evidence that clearly indicated that these witnesses would have put forward very strong evidence for the defense. Reverend Wood's wife would put in writing that

DR. FRANK BRYCE
TOOK PART IN TWO STORIES
COURTESY OF SARATOGA SPRINGS PUBLIC LIBRARY

HOME OF DR. C. S. GRANT
COURTESY OF SARATOGA SPRINGS PUBLIC LIBRARY

she had visited Ella each day during her illness. If she had testified before a jury there would have been even more reason to question Job's honesty, or at the very least his memory.

District Attorney Ormsby asked the judge to reject the defense's claim saying that the charges were over a month old and that the defense had had ample time to subpoena the witnesses.

Judge Lester reasoned that a trial could be held on at least one of the charges and ruled that the witnesses named were not important to the charge relating to Ella Lewis. It was ordered that Dr. Allen would stand trial on the one charge of failing to report to the Board of Health that Ella Lewis had a case of smallpox.

The prosecution put a very straightforward case. They wanted to prove that a well-publicized law existed that required anyone to report to the Board of Health a case of smallpox. An outside attorney, whose fee was paid by a member of the Board of Health, assisted District Attorney Ormsby. The two prosecutors put all three members of the Board of Health on the stand. Each testified that Dr. Allen had not reported any case of smallpox to them.

The prosecution then needed to prove that Ella had smallpox and that Dr. Allen knew that it was smallpox. They placed Dr. Boyce and Dr. Grant on the stand. Both of these doctors were allopathically trained. Both doctors were present when Ella's body was exhumed on

January 4th. Dr. Boyce was present because he was a member of the Board of Health. Dr. Grant was present because he was extremely respected within the community and had been brought in by Dr. Boyce. In all probability the twenty-five-year-old Boyce understood that his experience was at best weak. The two doctors noted that there were the telltale blotches associated with smallpox prevalent on Ella's body. Both doctors assured the jury that Ella had, in fact, died of smallpox. The two doctors maintained that any physician would be able to differentiate between small pox and chicken pox within six hours of the blotches appearing and a skilled doctor could tell even before a rash appeared on the skin.

It was now up to the prosecution to prove that Dr. Allen knew the cause of Ella's death. Although to both Drs. Grant and Boyce the symptoms were supposedly obvious, that did not mean that they were clear to Dr. Allen. The primary witness on this point was Job. The problem was that on each part of Job's testimony the defense had witnesses that would say clearly that he was incorrect. The problem was compounded by perception that the blotches may be less obvious on Ella as an African American. The prosecution's best evidence was the way the body was buried. The secrecy of Ella's death and her burial at night were hard to explain away. It was also the practice at the time to have the funeral of people who died of smallpox at night to avoid the possibility that the disease would spread.

The defense argued the case on several unrelated points. It was the defense's position that other portions of New York State law prohibited a doctor from disclosing a person's illness. They also put Miss Burt on the stand to say that Dr. Allen had stopped at Dr. Boyce's office to consult with him on Ella's case. Third, and of major significance, the defense would hold that Dr. Allen believed that Ella had chickenpox, not smallpox. There was no provision that a doctor needed to report a case of chickenpox. To add to the mixture the defense constantly tried to prove that Doctors Grant and Boyce were prejudiced against Dr. Allen because of his training. The two doctors both testified that they had no such prejudices. They also said under oath that they were not even aware of Dr. Allen's training. The position of the prosecution's doctors is hardly probable, as the two forms of medicine were in diametrically opposite and to believe in one was to dispute the other.

The defense had the advantage of witnesses that were residents of the house. They were able to put two respectable witnesses, Miss Burt and Camp, on the stand to say that Job was incorrect in his assertion that the room was locked and also about the appearance of the blotches.

The jury listened patiently as the lawyers made their closing arguments, both of which were as loaded with perceptions and innuendo as facts. The judge tried his best to provide the jury with the issues of law. Then the twelve men were left in the courtroom to try to determine Dr. Allen's guilt. The jury was out for almost twenty hours. When they began their deliberations they stood nine to three for conviction. After twelve hours the vote was eleven to one for conviction. For the final eight hours the remaining juror refused to change his vote. Finally, the judge was force to declare a mistrial. The judge ordered that Dr. Allen was to stand trial on all three charges in the next term (July) and dismissed the jury.

The defense asked the judge to release Dr. Allen on bail. The judge agreed with bail set at $5,000. Somehow in the confusion of the day, no one collected the bail and Dr. Allen was released. This oversight proved to be advantageous for Dr. Allen because in May the newspapers reported that Dr. Thomas Allen had sold his house to his brother, Asa, who also took over his practice. It was believed that Dr. Thomas Allen had sought a more suitable climate in Canada.

Newspapers were as quick to start, or in the very least, perpetuate rumors then as now. There was a story carried in the *Albany Argus* stating that an unnamed source, who was supposedly a friend of the one juror who had held out against a conviction, had made several bets at very favorable odds that the jury would be unable to reach a verdict.

***

There were several perplexing problems in the examination of this case. A hundred and twenty years later it is reasonable to assume that Ella died of smallpox and that at some point prior to her death Dr. Thomas Allen knew that she had the disease. Further he should have reported the cases to the Board of Health. He may have in a feeble way tried to contact Dr. Boyce, but why was he so reticent to inform the Board that there was an outbreak of a disease that had a nasty habit of appearing with some regularity? Assuming Dr. Allen was guilty, why did he hold off and insist on a trial? Was his reasoning that the death in his own house would have a negative impact on his proposed institute? The lawyers would say that the trial was a chance for the doctor to clear his reputation, which had been tarnished by the press.

The prosecution's case was even weaker than the defense's. First, the prosecution's case regarding what transpired in the boarding house rested exclusively on the testimony of one man, Job Lewis. There was significant testimony that Job was of limited mental ability. All the other witnesses, Fredrick Camp an architect, Miss Alice Burt, a teacher, and the Allen brothers, Asa and Thomas, were professional people each with their own reputation at stake. The district attorney was able to convince the judge to hold the trial while three of the defense's witnesses were unavailable. These witnesses included a minister, his wife and one of the housekeepers. These three had all submitted affidavits, which supported the position of the defense that there was no rash present on Ella until the Sunday before her death. These affidavits were not admitted, as the prosecution could not cross-examine on the facts presented. Why was the prosecution so anxious to avoid these reputable witnesses?

At least part of the answer to all of these questions rested in an understanding of the personality of the district attorney, Isaac Ormsby. Ormsby's work can be seen in the stories told in the books **To Spend Eternity Alone**, and in the Waterford bank robbery told in **Crimes In Time Vol. I**. Ormsby seems to have a trait whereby he

THE HOTEL LAFAYETTE - TOOK OVER DR. ALLEN'S
STOOD ON THE CORNER OF LAFAYETTE AND CIRCULAR UNTIL THE 1970'S
COURTESY OF SARATOGA SPRINGS PUBLIC LIBRARY

became locked in one logic. He was unable to escape from his perception of how events occurred long enough to reflect and see things from a different perspective. He also aligned himself with politically connected individuals such as Doctors Grant and Boyce.

Visiting the sites today
Green Ridge Cemetery

Once people gets over the admiration, brought on instantly by the numerous ostentatious monuments, on the top of the crest in Green Ridge Cemetery, they are ready to walk through this marble tribute to lives lived in different times. A stroll through this cemetery is equivalent to visiting an exhibit on the diversity in the class structure that existed in Victorian society. On the small hill are the grand tributes to lives passed and all too often not recorded. Along the side of the hill are those who owned businesses and were of the professional class. Spreading out we find the workers and journeymen. Along the fence on the east side of the cemetery are the graves of those who served the people who rest on the hill. Some of these lesser plots have only initials carved in simple stones. Some graves have no marker. The names of many, such as Ella Lewis, are gone forever; there affect on history may be as significant as Ella's, is now lost.

Dr. Allen's

The boarding house that Dr. Allen dreamed of transforming into a medical institute is gone. It stood on the southwest corner of Lafayette and Circular Street. After Dr. Asa Allen sold the building it remained a boarding house. Later it became the Lafayette Hotel, a kosher hotel. In the 1950s the building was still standing. Eventually, time and entropy took their toll and the building was torn down, replaced by a two-story home. The carriage house that Dr. Allen owned and from which he took his cutter that fateful night has been converted into a home. The building is on the north side of Lafayette Street, three buildings from the corner of Circular Street.

Dr. Grant's grand brick house stands on the corner of Walden and Woodlawn. In later years it was the Saratoga Elk's club.

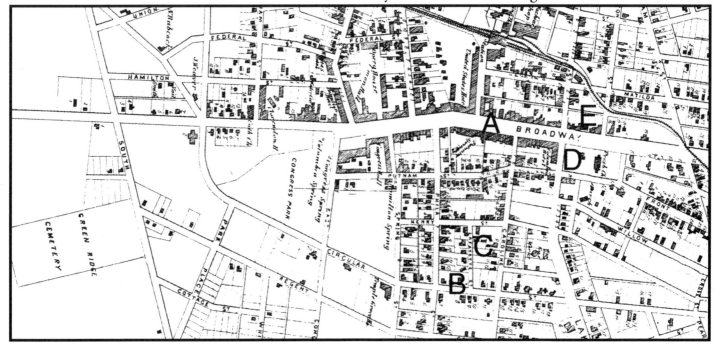

A. O'ROURKE'S SAMPLE ROOM SCENE OF THE SHOOTING
B. DR. ALLEN'S INSTITUTE
C. DR. ALLEN'S CARRIAGE HOUSE
D. CITY HALL
E. DR. REYNOLD'S OFFICE
SARATOGA COUNTY ATLAS 1866

The Shooting on Broadway

The blood ran freely from the face and chest of former Saratoga Springs Police Officer John McDermott. The injury that was only moments old was so disabling that a man named George Coon had to carry McDermott into the doctor's office. Although only a face wound was visible, the former constable was also suffering from a second wound to his chest. From the very beginning this was one of those cases where no one wanted to get involved. This was perhaps best demonstrated by the fact that George Coon's name never appeared again in the records. The name of the man who helped the injured man was probably fictitious.

DR. TABOR REYNOLDS
TREATED MCDERMOTT
COURTESY SARATOGA SPRINGS LIBRARY

Hearing a commotion, Dr. Tabor B. Reynolds left his private examining space and went into his waiting room where he saw the injured man. Dr. Reynolds' practice was on Broadway, which, even then, was one of the best addresses in Saratoga. The doctor asked McDermott what had caused the injury. Emotions were flying high and those in the room were busy trying to treat the injury. Among the turmoil they would report later that they thought they heard McDermott replied either, "I called O'Rourke a liar and he shot two balls at me." Or "O'Rourke fired two balls into my heart."

It appears Dr. Reynolds heard the comment about the injury being to the heart as he callously responded, "I guess not or you would not be living."

The wounded man was not to be dissuaded by the doctor's conclusion. Even in intense pain McDermott repeated his claim that he had taken two balls in his heart. Even wounded McDermott wanted to argue with the doctor's conclusion, saying words to the effect he had taken two balls to the heart, but this time he added that they would kill him.

Over the noise in the waiting room, the doctor repeated his assertion that the balls had not been to the heart. Rather than continue this foolish argument, the doctor started his treatment by examining the face wound. The reason for the facial examination being first was, in all probability, that the blood rushing from the face wound was clearly visible and the blood on McDermott's shirt could have been from the severe wound to the chin. The facial injury was described as a gash on the chin - an inch long and half-an-inch deep. The bullet that caused the facial wound continued on its course, causing a slight scratch on the man's neck. The doctor wrapped the jaw wound with a cloth bandage. In the same tradition as used during the Civil War, the bandage material was wrapped over the man's head. The way the doctor bound the wound was typical of the process used before adhesives. In this case the binding served a second purpose as it held McDermott's jaw closed,

THE HOME AND OFFICE OF DR. TABOR REYNOLDS
WHERE MCDERMOTT WENT FOR TREATMENT
FROM HISTORY OF SARATOGA COUNTY

thus ceasing the argument.

Believing that the man was telling the truth about being shot Dr. Reynolds looked at his chest. Opening the man's coat and shirt the doctor noted that the bullet had entered above the left nipple. This meant that the ball was in the area of the heart. He could see that there was sufficient blood oozing from breast wound and that it was serious. Realizing the gravity of the wound Dr. Reynolds sent for a second physician, Dr. Boyce, to help in the treatment. Conveniently, Dr. Boyce also happened to be the village coroner. The two doctors believed that the projectile had lodged in the neighborhood of, if not in, the man's lung. Reynolds spent approximately an hour treating the man's wounds. By that time, even with all that had been learned about treating gunshot wounds during the Civil War, there was nothing more the doctors could do for the patient. Dr. Reynolds arranged for transportation to take the man to his parents' home on Walnut Street.

When McDermott got home he lay on his bed for only a few minutes before he vomited blood. The end appeared inevitable.

***

Even when given a chance to straighten out his life, John McDermott was a man destined for trouble. McDermott had spent most of the years of his brief adult life living on the edge of discord. The previous April, in what was clearly a political exchange, he had been appointed as a village police officer. *The Saratoga Sentential* felt they were the watchdogs for the people. The newspaper ran an article relating to McDermott's appointment, and how the village trustees were being fair by patronizing petty criminals. It seems that McDermott had just been released from the county jail. He had served time for malicious mischief for "inking French Em's" house on Lake Avenue.

McDermott's tenure was brief as he was forced to resign the following fall. In those few months of service McDermott had been involved in a gambling scandal that had racked the peace and tranquility of Saratoga during the height of the season.

Saratoga Springs in the 1870s survived almost exclusively as a seasonal resort. There were some efforts to bring industry to the village (Saratoga was only a village at the time) but the efforts were greater than the rewards. As a resort it was essential that the village maintain the appearance of being a safe place to stay, even if that meant not reporting some of the more intriguing stories that were happening. Typical of Saratoga's scandals during the Victorian Era, little was written about the McDermott gambling incident while the story was evolving. It was only carried in the newspapers after the story had blown to such a magnitude that it was impossible to cover up.

In the 1870s as today horseracing was legal; however, other games of chance were not allowed including poker. Knowing the importance of keeping the community a vacation haven Saratoga officials generally ignored gambling as long as there was no cheating at the tables. In the summer of 1879 there was a problem the eventual outcome of which was the death of McDermott.

The Sting

In the summer of 1879 there was a clever sting operation going on in Saratoga. It was a time when the measure of a man could be made by his dress. Each day a well-dressed man, who will be called Mr. Net, and a woman, who at least portrayed herself as being his wife, would sit on the veranda of either the United States or the Grand Union Hotel. There they would strike up a conversation with some naive man, called Mr. Innocent, who was also enjoying the weather on the portico. While they were conversing another man, Mr. Sting, would come up and act like a friend of Mr. Net's. Mr. Sting would tell how he had just lost over $200 at the track. Mr. Sting would project himself as being an imprudent fellow, saying that he was going across Broadway to one of the "dens" to bet his last $50. It was either win back his stake or go home. He would invite Mr. Net to join him. After a little convincing Mr. Net would agree so long as his new acquaintance, Mr. Innocent, was also invited to watch.

Being the rowdy one, Mr. Sting would agree to the additional companionship.

The three men would then all walk across Broadway. In the dark rooms that were the casinos of there times, Mr. Sting would miraculously win a couple of hands. Having won back his afternoon losses, he would flip five dollars in chips to both Mr. Net and Mr. Innocent so that they could try their luck. Inevitably they would both win the first couple of times. Then the cards would turn. If the operation was set up right and the right mark had been spotted Mr. Innocent would leave minus a hundred dollars or more.

The scheme worked for some time until two the marks were sitting on the veranda one afternoon, instead of going to the track. As they began to converse about why they couldn't afford to go the track, they realized that they had both been the victim of the same sting. They two men who had been taken in by the scam reported it to the authorities.

Action is Taken

In July 1879, during the peak of the summer season there were social reformers at work in Saratoga Springs. Justice Charles Lester was one of the men who wanted Saratoga to be a morally safe place for visitors, or at the very least he wanted them treated fairly when they were engaging in illegal activities. Hearing about the scam, on the eleventh of the month Justice Lester issued four warrants relating to gambling in the village. One set was for the confiscation of gambling equipment that was being used in a "den" at number 3 Washington Street to arrest the proprietor of the property, a man known as Drummery. The second set was for an establishment on Broadway, operated by a man named Meyers.

The warrants were given to Chief of Police George Adams and Deputy John McDermott to be acted upon. Adams and McDermott went to the Washington Street "Den" intent on "pulling" the equipment. They did not arrest anyone, although when they went inside there was a man presiding at the gambling table. The warrant was

for the arrest of Drummery but the Chief, for reasons never clarified, said that he thought the warrant was for a man named Lane. When Chief Adams asked the man at the gambling table if his name was Lane he said quiet honestly no. It was at this juncture that the corruption in the police force became evident. The man was in fact Drummery and he was not arrested.

Adams and McDermott "pulled" the equipment from the Washington Street establishment and took it in a trunk to the janitor's closet in the new village hall on the corner of Broadway and Lake Avenue (the same building and location as today). The two officers never acted on the warrants for the Broadway "den" or Meyers.

***

Late in the afternoon of July 19th, Police Officer B. Thayer Bacon saw McDermott walk into the Lake Avenue entrance to Village Hall. It

JUDGE CHARLES S. LESTER
PRESIDED OVER INVESTIGATION INTO
MCDERMOTT'S DEATH
COURTESY SARATOGA SPRINGS PUBLIC LIBRARY

had been a little over a week since the "pulling of the equipment" on Washington Street. Wanting to talk to McDermott, Bacon followed him in the door but was unable to find him inside the building. After looking for fifteen minutes, Bacon was about to give up the search when he saw McDermott and Chief Adams come out of the janitor's closet and walk up the stairs to the main entrance. It was later that evening that Bacon heard that the gambling equipment that had been pulled from Drummery had been stolen from the janitor's closet at Village Hall.

Later the same day Ira Morrison, the same constable in the story *The Man of Many Names*, was sitting on the steps of the American Hotel in Ballston Spa. He saw a wagon with Adams and Drummery pull up to the express office. Knowing both men by sight, and having heard about the raid on Drummery's establishment the previous week, he thought it peculiar that they were together. His inquisitiveness aroused, Morrison watched as the two unlikely colleagues unloaded a trunk and took it into the express office.

After the two men left, Morrison went into the office and asked the agent about the trunk. Shown the trunk but not its contents, Morrison noted that it was to be shipped to an address in Albany.

When the gambling equipment was initially reported missing from Village Hall, Justice

VILLAGE HALL SARATOGA SPRINGS
LOOKS MUCH THE SAME TODAY AS IN 1881
THE SIDE DOOR ON LAKE WAS USED BY MCDERMOTT TO ENTER
THE MAIN ENTRANCE WAS USED TO SMUGGLE OUT THE GAMBLING APARATUS

Lester stepped aside knowing that he had issued the initial warrants. The case was turned over to Justice Barrett. Barrett was delighted when Morrison walked into his office and told him what he had learned. Barrett began a very public inquiry that was attended by members of the press. After Officers Bacon and Morrison had given their testimony before Barrett a special meeting of the village trustees was called. After minimal review Adams and McDermott were suspended without pay pending a hearing on the matter.

Adams never testified before Barrett and the village counsel dismissed him at the next regular meeting. McDermott did testify, but it was probably more damaging than if he had just accepted his dismissal. It came out that McDermott had tried to intimidate Morrison into not testifying. It seems that Adams had spotted Morrison the night of the delivery to the express office. McDermott was sent to see if Morrison was going to rat on a fellow officer. In the conversation between McDermott and Morrison, McDermott allegedly admitted to taking the equipment for $60.

***

Village elections are in March. At the meeting to start the new trustees, McDermott's initial appointment to the police force had been part of a political trade. The president of the Board of Trustees (a position equivalent to mayor today) of the village of Saratoga had allegedly traded his vote, thereby supporting McDermott for the backing of Trustee John Leary for other areas in the Republican agenda. Leary would be both McDermott's mentor and, in a small part, the reason for his having been shot.

In an interesting side twist, Leary's brother was appointed lamplighter for the village at the same meeting. The appointment of the brother turned out to be fodder for the village scandal machine. When the brother turned in a bill for fifty dollars for one month's service, Trustee Boyce (yes, the same Boyce as from the Dr. Allen story and the coroner brought in at the beginning of this story) raised an uproar, claiming the price was

exorbitant. For two months the debate over the lamplighter's fee raged in the newspapers. Eventually, it was decided that the position of lamplighter should be bid out. Another man won the bid when he agreed to only charge the city $35 a month. Reading the accounts of the trustees meeting shows that the politics of old differed only slightly from those of today. Elected officials would show their interest in the public's tax dollar over fifteen dollars a month and let the $5,000, allotted to newly appointed Chief of the Fire Department O'Rourke, go unquestioned.

In sharp contrast to the life of McDermott was that of Michael O'Rourke. O'Rourke and his brother Patrick, who went by "B", owned O'Rourke's Sample Room. The phrase sample room was a dressed up name for a tavern. O'Rourke's establishment was at 449 Broadway in Saratoga Springs. At the same trustees meeting where McDermott and Adams had been appointed to the police department, O'Rourke had been promoted to chief engineer in the fire department. In today's terminology the engineer has been dropped and O'Rourke would be considered the chief of the village's fire department. For an Irish man enduring the biases of the 1880s, O'Rourke had attained a very high and rightly deserved status. Although one newspaper called the connection "O'Rourke's machine." This term was probably based on the number of appointed city employees who could be found in the O'Rourke's Sample Room.

The Problem Between O'Rourke and McDermott

began the Saturday night prior to the shooting. McDermott, who was now scratching a living as a day worker, had decided to patronize O'Rourke's bar where he intended to play some cards and have a few drinks.

O'Rourke's Sample Room was divided into three distinct sections, separated from each other by wooden lattes work. When someone entered from Broadway they were in an area set up to sell cigars and other smoking paraphernalia. The sec-

70

THE O'ROURKE SAMPLE HOUSE WAS IN THE BUILDING MARKE WITH AN "O"
PUBLISHED AND DRAWN BY L. R. BURLEIGH, TROY, N. Y. 1884

ond section was the bar and the third was set up with tables on which the customers could play cards. In the first room there was a glass counter to the left (south), which served as a humidor. Across the room were kegs of beer and casks of whiskey stacked against the wall. There were two openings from the first room to the second. One was behind the counter and led to the area behind the bar. This doorway allowed whoever was working the bar to also wait on customers in the smoking area. The second doorway was for the customers. Between the first and second sections, there were the customary swinging doors made famous in western movies. The second or center section had a bar, and was equipped with a woodstove that heated the entire saloon. In the winter, which is when this story takes place, the swinging doors were often fixed back to let the heat circulate throughout the pub.

The blindfold worn by Victorian Society contained enough space so that men could condemn gambling institutions, yet those same individuals would think nothing of engaging in a game of cards among friends at the local watering hole. Gambling was only wrong if others did it as an occupation or you lost a lot of money. McDermott had gone to O'Rourke's on the night of December 13th. Ostensibly he was there to play cards with his friends. After a couple of hours of drinks without playing any cards an argument broke out between McDermott and his mentor John Leary, who had been drinking and was playing cards. One of the patrons attempted unsuccessfully to mediate, telling the two men to "set down." For a moment the two accepted the outside interference. The peace was short lived, as McDermott and Leary were too frustrated with each other to let the matter rest. In minutes they resumed their argument. McDermott jumped up and threatened to "kick" Leary.

As the owners, Mike O'Rourke and his brother had to step in. He told the men to take their argument outside. Both men left the bar peacefully enough. Being kicked out was an event all too customary for a man with a reputation like McDermott; however, it was quite uncommon in O'Rourke's place, as it was considered to be a quiet social establishment. To everyone else in the bar that night what happened was just a minor incident, one that would have soon been forgotten, if only McDermott had let it lay. Outside, whatever anger McDermott had for Leary shifted to O'Rourke. A few minutes later another customer walked into the smoking room. While the door was open McDermott's voice could be heard yelling in, "O'Rourke come out here."

O'Rourke responded calmly enough, "Go away and shut that door."

"O'Rourke, you don't dare to come out here. You're a __ coward." McDermott responded. McDermott kept up the verbal barrage calling O'Rourke abusive names such as "coward, sucker" and "duffer" (as strong language as they would print in the newspapers).

O'Rourke tired of McDermott's antics and told him to leave the area or he would call a police officer and have him arrested. McDermott either went away or went quiet for a few minutes. However, five minutes later McDermott returned to outside the sample room and to his former behavior.

"I'll give it to you, you ____, wherever I meet you!" Taking one last breath McDermott added, "I'll down you."

An un-raddled O'Rourke said, "No you won't."

The matter could have and should have ended at this point. Unfortunately, for McDermott he wasn't able to let go. Three nights later a friend of McDermott's, James Kearney (also spelled Carney in some of the newspapers), also had trouble at O'Rourke's. Like McDermott, Kearney had been asked to leave. Unlike McDermott, Kearney had been so drunk he was unclear about what happened. Like McDermott, Kearney was holding a grudge over what had occurred.

James Kearney was a porter at the National Waterbury Hotel in Saratoga. As part of his duties he transported passengers and their luggage to the train terminal at the corner of Division and Terminal Streets. On the morning of December 17th, Kearney had taken a load of baggage for the 10:00 southbound train. After he brought a few off-season passengers back to the hotel, Kearney met McDermott on Broadway. The meeting between the friends in front of a cigar store was not purely by coincidence. At nine the morning of December 16th, McDermott heard of Kearney's problems at O'Rourke's place the night before. McDermott told the man who had told him about the incident that he and Kearney would go down to O'Rourke's and "throw the Irish __ __ __ __ out and open a free house for the boys." The fact that Kearney had scratches on his face that he could not account for, added fire to the fuel of hatred that was building in both men.

It was well out of the season in Saratoga so both Kearney and McDermott knew that the other could use a little extra spending money, but that the prospects of finding work were slim. They decided that they would go to the new office of a mutual friend, "Judge" Michael Berrigan. In fairness Berrigan had only recently passed the bar so where the nickname Judge came from is very unclear. They were hoping that Berrigan could use their help setting up his new office in Ainseworth Place. After visiting with Berrigan for about ten minutes, McDermott and Kearney realized that they were not going to get any work. Frustrated, the two-day workers decided to leave Berrigan's office. Always the first to propose a drink, McDermott suggested to both men present, "Let's go and have a drink."

It was only slightly after 10:30 in the morning so Berrigan begged off. Kearney, however, took McDermott up on his suggestion. The two crossed to the west side of Broadway where they had a drink in a bar. This was the beginning of a very heavy binge. In each of the places mentioned the revel rousers had at least one drink of hard liquor except when they went to the spring. From the tavern on the west side of Broadway the men went to a nearby stable in search of others who may want to spend the day in foolish folly. They had a drink directly from the bottle at the stable then went to a bar under the Adelphi Hotel. From there they went down to the Hawthorn Spring. They then went to O'Rourke's where Mike's brother "B" O'Rourke allowed them to have a drink. By the time they were at O'Rourke's it was almost noon. They then went back to the Adelphi bar. They returned to the stable again looking for a friend named Callahan. The growing group now went to the Continental Hotel where they had a couple of drinks. McDermott and Callahan stayed at the Continental for lunch, which they pushed down with more drinks.

By this time it was late enough for the men to begin drinking more seriously. They went to a tavern across from the train station and drank heavily while they waited for a train to take Mike Callahan north. After Callahan left the men decided that travel would be a good idea and set off for Dublin. They got the one block from the terminal to Division Street when they decided that Ireland would have to await their company, and so they opted to go back and settle the score with O'Rourke.

There were only three of the group left by the time they reached O'Rourke's Sample Room for the second time that day. The three were James Kearney, Jack Driscoll and James McDermott. They entered the first room where Kearney saw the former police chief, George Adams, in the cigar area. Kearney stopped to have a conversation with Adams. He was heard to ask Adams, "Do you know how these scratches came to be on my face?" Driscoll and McDermott continued into the bar area where Driscoll asked, "Mike, give the boys something."

O'Rourke placed a bottle on the bar and said, "Jack, you can have anything you want. But them other fellows can't have nothing. I wont wait on the other party." No names were actually used; the assumption of everyone present was that O'Rourke was referring to Kearney and McDermott. After pausing while he got a glass on the bar O'Rourke added, "I don't want them in my house."

Driscoll tried to mitigate the situation saying, "Mike I don't want a drink, I want a smoke." As O'Rourke reached for the bottle intent on returning it to its place under the bar, McDermott reached around Driscoll, grabbing the bottle and saying, "You Irish ___ __ __ __, I'll have some drink any way." With that McDermott turned the bottle upside down and began to pour a small portion of the contents onto the floor.

O'Rourke didn't respond. He just started to walk through the opening in the lattice partition. Driscoll realized that O'Rourke was after his pistol or a club and went through the customer opening to get behind the counter and grab O'Rourke. By the time Driscoll had gotten around the counter to the opening that was used by the bartender, O'Rourke had the pistol in hand. O'Rourke started back into the bar area through the employee opening, just as McDermott's was coming out of the bar into the cigar area through the customer opening. When McDermott went through the customer entrance he did not go for the outside door. Instead he went for a pitcher of water. The difference between Driscoll's actions and McDermott was that, Driscoll was trying to prevent any further problem, while McDermott was moving to keep the action going.

McDermott was holding the bottle by the neck when he pulled it back over his shoulder. Those who could see could not determine at that moment whether he intended to throw the bottle or use it as a club. In either event the contents were spilling onto the floor.

O'Rourke came back into the opening and started to raise the pistol, pointing it at McDermott. Driscoll called out, "For God's sake Mike don't shoot." Although O'Rourke had already grabbed the gun, Driscoll was able to grasp O'Rourke's arms to his chest in a rough bear hug. At that same moment that Driscoll got hold of O'Rourke he felt something break over his head. He couldn't see what it was, but

McDermott had thrown the bottle at O'Rourke's just missing his head. The glass bottle smashed on the frame with shatters of glass falling onto both Driscoll and O'Rourke. The bottle was thrown with such force that it left an indentation in the wooden frame.

McDermott pulled back the pitcher to throw it at McDermott when there were three shoots fired. In an instant, Driscoll wrestled O'Rourke back into the bar area. By now the commotion was too much to totally clarify. Driscoll remembered asking O'Rourke, "Mike, what have you done?"

Mike O'Rourke turned to Driscoll and said, "Jack, you've saved my life."

Driscoll went into the cigar area to check on McDermott. That is when he learned that McDermott had already left for the doctor's office.

From the angle of the wounds it would appear that the first shot hit McDermott in the chest. At that point he either leaned forward so the second struck him diagonally in the face, or more likely, when Driscoll wrestled O'Rourke backward one of the shots went up ricocheting off the ceiling into McDermott's face and neck. The third shell was found the next day, laying on one of the unopened kegs.

***

When the newspaper heard about the story of a shooting on Broadway they sent one of the reporters to check for details. The reporter went immediately to O'Rourke's to ask what had occurred. To his surprise, O'Rourke was still at the bar. The reporter noted that after having just shot a man they found O'Rourke "somewhat excited and a trifle pale."

When the reporter asked if McDermott was under the influence of alcohol when he entered the bar, O'Rourke was slow to answer. Several of his associates who were in the now closed tavern assured the reporter that McDermott had been drinking the entire day. The reporter asked what happened and O'Rourke responded to the facts with reasonable accuracy. O'Rourke was already prepared for his defense, if one were to become necessary, when he was quot-

ed as saying, "I was bound to protect myself and property."

The reporter questioned several other people in the bar and they all assured him that the report given by Chief O'Rourke was accurate. They did add one thing that the chief had not put in and that was that they were all sure that McDermott had come into the bar intent on "serious mischief."

A short while later Chief O'Rourke surrendered himself to one of the village police officers. The officer felt that since O'Rourke had not run it would be safe to allow him to return to his house on Front Street for the night. The officer was right. O'Rourke was home in the morning when the officer went to pick him up and take him before the police justice.

O'Rourke had retained two counselors, Pike and Foley, who had recently served with the prosecution in the Billings trial. To everyone

ATTORNEY JOHN FOLEY
DEFENDER OF O'ROURKE
COURTESY OF SARATOGA SPRINGS LIBRARY

present O'Rourke seemed cool and collected as the justice read the warrant sworn out by McDermott's father. The warrant that was issued stated:

Whereas, Complaint has this day been made by Terence McDermott on oath before me, Police Justice of the village of Saratoga Springs in said county, that Michael O'Rourke of the town of Saratoga Springs, in said county, on or about the 16th day of December 1879, at the town of Saratoga Springs, in said county has been guilty of feloniously shooting at John McDermott of said village with a certain revolver pistol loaded with gunpowder and lead with intent to kill the said John McDermott, against the peace of the people of the State of New York, and it appearing there from that the said offense has been committed you are therefore commanded forthwith to take the said O'Rourke and bring him before me, the said police Justice to be dealt with according to law.

***

Later in the evening of the shooting the doctor had visited with McDermott at his parents' house where he found him failing. During the night McDermott's father had gone for Dr. Reynolds again. At this juncture the doctor was reasonably sure that McDermott's wounds were going to prove fatal.

When the justice asked for a plea he was told through the retained counsel that O'Rourke was pleading "not guilty". The justice began a preliminary hearing on the charge, calling the doctor to the stand. Part way through the justice's questioning of the doctor, an attorney came, stating that he was in the room on behalf of the district attorney. The attorney for the people said that pending McDermott's condition the most that should be held was a preliminary hearing.

The justice called Kearney to the stand to give a brief statement as to what had occurred.

Then the justice ordered Coroner Boyce to go get a statement regarding the affair from McDermott. The statement of a person on the verge of death was called an ante-mortem statement. An ante-mortem statement was only given if the person understood that he or she were going to die. These statements were usually considered to be absolutely true since, who would want to meet his maker with a lie fresh on his lips. Understanding what was expected Boyce went to McDermott and told him of his "precarious" condition. McDermott assured the doctor that he was right and that he did not expect to live. The doctor then recorded this brief ante-mortem statement:

Kearney, Driscoll and myself went into Michael O'Rourke's to get a drink; had had some words with O'Rourke the night before; he would not give us anything to drink; we had some words and he shot me twice; afterwards I took two pitchers and threw them at him; after being shot I walked out and went to Dr. Reynolds's office with a young man; at the time of our previous trouble there were no threats made by either of us.

McDermott's recollection of what had happened differed from every other witness who appeared on the stand or was quoted in the newspaper. In fairness, and not to say that a dying man lied, it should be noted that McDermott might have had so much to drink that he was unclear about what had occurred.

At 2:15 the afternoon after the shooting, after twenty-three hours of pain, John McDermott died.

This was a time when the newspapers felt that they had the right to remind people how to behave. *The Daily Saratogian* reminded its readers as follows:

John McDermott, who died yesterday, leaves a father, mother and sister residing here. It is unnecessary to say that they are in deep grief over the result of Tuesday's shooting. They certainly deserve the sympathy of the public.

The next morning, December 18th, the charge against O'Rourke had been modified adding, "it appearing that said offence has been committed." That inquest began at four that afternoon and continued until almost midnight. The night ended with a witness named Harvey Cook. Cook said that during the shooting he had been in the front room (cigar area) of the sample room. According to Cook, after the bottle was thrown and the first shot was fired, he grabbed McDermott. This was at about the same time that Driscoll had grabbed O'Rourke. He went on to say that McDermott became passive in his grasp. Even while being held, O'Rourke fired two shots. These were the ones that struck McDermott. Every other witness said Cook was in the bar section not in the cigar area.

The small police court in the village hall was filled to capacity until the close of the inquiry that evening. Not all the witness had been called, so the justice postponed the remainder of the hearing until the following evening.

Those who gathered at 8:00 the second evening were disappointed by what happened next. O'Rourke's counsel advised the court that they felt that an incident that had resulted in the death of a man required a grand jury. They then waived the preliminary hearing. The justice denied the request, stating that he needed to make a finding as to cause of death. The coroner's jury found that O'Rourke was not guilty, as the shooting was done in self-defense. They then went further, reprimanding James Kearney for not trying to prevent the incident.

***

The case did not end at this juncture. The district attorney felt that he could support a charge of manslaughter, so he had O'Rourke arrested and brought to the county seat in Ballston Spa. The next day a judge held a hearing regarding bail for O'Rourke. The judge set bail at $5,000. Immediately some well-known Saratoga businessmen put their names on a bond, assuring that they would pay in the event O'Rourke failed to appear. The judge was satisfied that sufficient signatures were present. The defense was not content and went out and had nine more names added. Among the names added later were the state assemblyman and two of the wealthiest men in Saratoga.

Less than a month later the grand jury concluded its investigation. On January 11th, the grand jury voted unanimously that no charges were warranted against O'Rourke. O'Rourke was a free man because under Victorian Rules you had a right to protect yourself by the use of fatal force, and if the person you killed didn't deserve to live you were providing a public service by ending their life.

Visiting the Site Today

Unfortunately most of the old hotels are gone. The building on the corner of Broadway and Washington may be the one that where the gambling equipment was "pulled". The City Hall on the corner of Lake and Broadway is the same building from which Officer McDermott and Chief Adams smuggled out the gambling equipment.

The site of the shooting is now a store called Suave Faire. Although this is not the same building, if one were inside and before the stairs to the platform area they are in the area where the argument broke out. McDermott was shot in the area of the front entrance.

McDermott made it up the street to the doctor's office on Broadway. The office is now a flower shop. Somehow a flower shop replacing a doctor's office is a fitting ending.

76

Interlude

Since few people actually read a preface that does not mean that some major points usually covered therein should not be addressed. To deal with the issue an interlude was created to cover the topics usually at the beginning of a work of non-fiction. This was done in the hope that by the time readers reached this point in the book they might actually want to learn more about the research and other issues involved in the book's creation.

This interlude was done in a question and answer format. Some of the questions are the common ones that arise during presentations done over the course of a year.

How can there be quotes in a true crime book?

The crimes in the various books published by Deep Roots Publications were often the biggest news in their community the decade they occurred. Since they all happened during the Victorian Era, the timing was excellent for the collection of background information. After the Civil War two significant events linked. If only on a limited scale, the majority of people were able to read. Because of better transportation and equipment, printing costs had been greatly reduced. Therefore, for the first time, the primary source of news was the local newspaper(s). The community's interest in these cases sold the local newspapers. The best example is that when the articles about the Rowell/Lynch murder were carried in The Batavia News, the publishers tripled their circulation, with many of the papers sold in Utica.

Publishers recognized the economic impact of writing about a local crime. As a general rule the newspapers took one of two reporting styles. They either printed as much information as possible to keep the people reading or they took an opinion/political stand using controversy to sell newspapers. In the former the accounts often came very close to being verbatim testimony or at the very least a close paraphrasing. It is from these accounts that the conversations can be determined with reasonable accuracy. In the case where controversy was the catalyst one can learn the opinion of the opposing sides within the community.

The real advantage in researching these crimes as compared to those of today is they happened before the invention of radio and television, which have reduced American journalism to a 90-second sound bite.

Where do the stories come from and why didn't people know about them before?

The Victorian Era in America came primarily after the Civil War. At that time much of the public's interest in adventure was focused on the perception of a great-untamed West. The daring crimes there became the subject of dime novels with antiheroes such as the James brothers. In reality the crimes committed in the West were often dwarfed by some of the crimes that took place in the East. There are of course the famous crimes in the east such as the murder of Lizzie Borden's parents or the murder of Sanford White.

There are a multitude of sources that have led to the discovery of the many crimes that have been reported. Just determining that there is a crime does not mean that it was interesting enough to actually be retold. The information necessary for the stories that appeared in the various volumes came from the following:

•In the research from other stories – often in the columns on one story a reporter would cite a previous crime that was in some way related to the one that is being researched.

•New York Times Index – This is one of the most important sources. Although the Times never carried a story in detail, they published an index of the cases it covered.

•Readers who tell of a story they know about. Two retired judges, who are regular readers of these books, best exemplified this process. They have related stories such as one where bank robbers were caught in a dip in the road during an ice storm and couldn't get out and the police could not get down to arrest them.

•*The Police Gazette* – During most of the Victorian Era there was a weekly newspaper entitled *The*

Police Gazette. It was considered a barbershop periodical, since that was where it could be found and discussed. The *Gazette's* coverage was often little more than a brief outline but provided key dates.

•Obituaries of trial lawyers – It wasn't until the second book that it was discovered that the obituaries of trial lawyers would be an outstanding source of cases. This was especially true for defense attorneys as they only listed the cases they were noted for winning not their losses.

No one should think that any of these sources was ever the complete source of the story that was written. These sources only opened the door to months of research.

What are the primary sources used in the research for the stories?

The newspapers of the period, historical societies, and museums are the main source of information. Each provides a different resource. Newspapers provide what was believed on a given date. By examining the articles on one case over the entire period from the incident of the crime until the conclusion of the trial a great many perceptions can be seen and often they change. Historical societies and museums provide pictures, and background. The problem is that the background is usually on the peripheral characters.

What are the problems with writing true crime period pieces?

The biggest obstacle to the research is finding the dates. Hours have been spent looking at the screen on a microfilm reader trying to find out when a trial began or worse yet a retrial – these were usually years later.

The second problem is in understanding the values of the period. The 1870s is a classic example of this problem. Ten years before the country had been ripped apart by a civil war. Yet they tried to come together for the great centennial celebration in 1876 held in Philadelphia. During this period there were waves of immigration and the transcontinental railroad opened the area west of the Mississippi to development. The country was going from being almost exclusively a Protestant, English, or at the most, western European homeland, to one that was truly multicultural. Understanding the evolving conflicts and their effect on justice takes time.

Is this type of writing profitable?

So far the four books that have been published have just about broken even. The work continues for a variety of reasons that are not economic.

•Most important is the belief that keeping people interested in history is a worthwhile endeavor. It is always fascinating when relating a story, in the vicinity of where it occurred, how few people knew anything about what had happened. If future generations are to be interested in history the focus needs to shift to the human element. History needs to be told more through the tales of real people.

•Trying to solve a hundred-year-old mystery is fun. Some people enjoy playing sports or have some other hobby. This is mine and it keeps me from committing a similar crime.

•The presentations done on the books are interesting. One favorite pastime is when asked to be a storyteller or presenter for some organization.

Would a more modern story be undertaken?

It is highly unlikely that, as an author of non-fiction, a story would be undertaken that was not from the Victorian Era. The reason is simple. It is very difficult to become truly knowledgeable about the events and values of any given period. The economy has always run in cycles. These cycles impact people and their perceptions. There are also regional differences that create a background for each story. During the research on this book it was discovered that Batavia grew by over fifty percent in two years. It doesn't matter where you are, that level of growth spurs opportunity but also creates difficulties. Similarly, there was a negative emotional impact in places that were not growing or perhaps even experiencing a declining population.

Why an interest in the Victorian Era?

The Victorian Era is a fascination because it is such a classic example of divergent values existing in imperfect harmony. We are led to believe that the Victorian Era was a better, safer time to have lived. In point of fact this period is the epitome of a society living in a state of total hypocrisy. One always attended religious services on Sunday even if they had spent the evening before in a gambling den, house of ill repute or tavern. Although we wanted it to be a time when we lived the good life what was really important was that we appeared to live such life.

The Victorian Era was a time of absolutes. Women were either fast or pure. Men stood up for their rights or were weak. Fathers and brothers protected the women of the family yet frequented houses of ill repute. The men, when in the house, seemed as if they did not realize that the women employed therein were someone else's sister or daughter.

It was a time long before the concept of political correctness. It was accepted and even expected that people could be judged by their national origin, color of their skin, or by if their fortunes were improving – surely no fair God would allow an evil man to become wealthy on earth. Similarly a man who fell on hard times did so because of some failing of his own.

The small segment of society that was rich was extremely rich, and those in this select group tried to outshine each other by living lavishly. At the same time the far larger group that was poor struggled to survive. As with all periods of society that is growing and improving, the middle class was expanding. The professional men on whom the outcome of many of these stories rest, left a deep and unrecorded legacy that it takes time to grasp.

How the conflicts of Victorian values affected individuals is probably best exemplified by the story *Too Many Barbers*. Pair knew his fifteen-year-old daughter had been in a sexual relationship with her own uncle. He understood that public knowledge of this relationship would condemn her to a life on the fringes of society. Given the limited choices at his disposal, Pair said in a letter that if the uncle would marry the daughter it would make things right. One can only hope that in small towns today we have moved away from so few options.

One of the other elements of the Victorian Era that must be enjoyed was that it was a social period. People lived on farms, in hamlets and villages, only a few lived in cities. For better or for worse a person knew their neighbors. Heroes were local not national. The acceptable boundaries of society were so narrowly defined. People could walk to the nice neighborhoods or drive their wagons quickly through those that were less desirable. Without the traps of TV and the Internet, people went out at night. People didn't watch their children alone; the upbringing of the young was a community's responsibility.

At this time children came home to do chores while today children are chores. People have since redefined childhood to be an organized period. For good or ill gone are the days when a group of kids picked teams and a ball game would go on for hours. Now they either are on organized teams or they sit at home grazing through the Internet, playing video games or gazing mindlessly at television.

During the Victorian Era times were harder but they were also truer. People knew where they stood. Unfortunately, unless they were willing to move they rarely were able to move from that one strata of society.

What's next?

In writing this book a story was uncovered where a jealous wife attempted to shoot her husband's mistress. It was fully researched and was being written when a second story involving a woman was heard of. The second story was of a woman in Troy who was called the veiled murderess. Again the research was taken on. Then the idea of a book relating only crimes committed by women was born. Both stories were temporarily put aside to be used in next year's book **The Crimes in Times Journal III - Leave it to the Ladies**. This book is scheduled to be out in time for the Traver's in Saratoga.

There is also a story in development that is terribly intriguing. That murder involves three U.S. senators, a general who was a war hero and several judges. It is uncertain at this time whether this will be a stand-alone book, or part of **Crimes in Time Journal IV.** To tell the story properly it may need to be a book by itself.

There is also an evolution into storytelling. Over the course of the last few years the author has been called upon to tell these stories to groups or as something equivalent to dinner theater.

Why the Title Victorian Rules?

In this volume the person who committed the crime is almost always known. The reason they were not sent to prison was the way their crime was perceived under the Victorian values in place at the time. Thus they were playing under Victorian Rules.

The Man of Many Names

There are some crime stories that really would be of little consequence if it were not that they have a unique or unusual twist. In fact some become more and more bizarre as the circumstances develop. This is exactly what happened in the case known as "The Man of Many Names."

In the middle of the afternoon of August 18, 1879, a middle-aged man whose appearance implied he was of dubious character appeared in the streets of the village of Ballston Spa. He started his endeavors that day at a small hotel known as the Ballston Spa House. His adventure began when he walked into the lobby and immediately went up to the desk clerk and asked for a blank paper. He justified his presence in the village by telling the clerk that he was employed by W. A. "Billy" Collamer. Collamer just happened to be the supervisor for the town of Malta, a rural area east of the village. The man offered to pay for the paper as soon as he caught up with Collamer. The man was told that he could find paper on a stand in the lobby. Instead of the single sheet he had asked for the man took several sheets. The suspicious clerk monitored the man's movements, noting that he went to a small table and wrote on one of the sheets. To offend the clerk even more the man used the hotel's ink without asking.

After the man had written a message on at least one of the sheets, he then moved his "business" down the street to the Eagle Hotel, which stood on the corner of Front Street and Milton Avenue. He walked up to the clerk and asked him to accept a handwritten note referred to as a "due bill." This was the period before checks so as a payment people would often write a due bill, which worked like a check. These notes were often signed over to others as payments. The clerk observed the bill, which was for between twenty and thirty dollars, and signed by W. A. Collamer. When asked where he obtained the note, the man said he had accepted it as payment of a personal debt from a milk peddler in Saratoga. The stranger's nature did not inspire the clerk's confi-

dence in such a transaction. Wisely, the clerk decided to compare the signature on the bottom of the note to one of Collamer's on the hotel's register. Apparently Mr. Collamer had stayed at the hotel, which was less than a six-mile ride from his home (but that is a set of circumstances that we don't know). The hotel clerk seemed to relish the opportunity of informing the man the signatures didn't match. In rejecting the note the clerk went so far as to declare the signature "spurious."

Not one to give up a rouse easily, the man then tried to push the note on other business establishments around Ballston Spa. The man first moved his efforts to Henry's Clothing Store. At the store his approach changed slightly. Where before he wanted cash, now he was willing to accept some goods with the remainder of the note in cash. He milled around the store for some time selecting items he could use. When asked the nature of his business he told the clerk he was waiting for Mr. Collamer. After a time the man asked the clerk to accept Mr. Collamer's note for the clothes and give him change. The store clerk refused the "gracious" offer.

Getting frustrated the man walked down the street to the bar at the Commercial Hotel. He asked the bartender to accept the note; again he was trying for cash. He had no way of knowing that the bartender was the owner's son. The son wasn't inclined to take a chance on his family's money. The bartender noted that the note was for $26.80. This in a time when families were living on five to eight dollars a week. Being a man that would not want to discourage a potentially affluent customer the bartender suggested that the man try making the exchange at the livery.

The man took a short detour on the way to the livery, stopping at a local grocery store. He started by showing the owner the note suggesting that he take five dollars in trade and the rest in cash. Again the man was turned down.

Sensing that time was becoming his enemy, the man went to the livery. Again he changed his

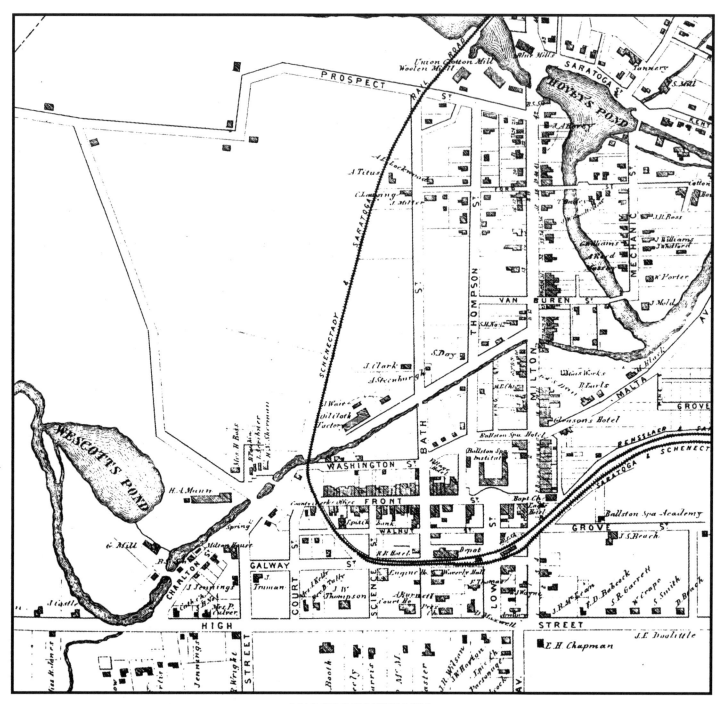

MAP OF BALLSTON SPA
ATLAS OF SARATOGA COUNTY 1866

approach this time telling the boy who worked in the stable that he wanted to rent a horse to go see Mr. Collamer. He handed the boy the note to see if he would take it as payment for rental of a horse. Before the man could stop him, the boy was out the door in search of the owner to see if the note was acceptable.

At the time Ira Morrison was a constable in Ballston Spa. In the early afternoon, Morrison had gotten "a whisper" that something was amiss. Hearing a description of the man, the constable could remember seeing him walking from the Eagle Hotel to the clothing store. It didn't take Morrison long to ascertain that the man was in the livery.

As Morrison approached the livery the man was standing in the stable doorway awaiting the boy's return with his note. Looking out the

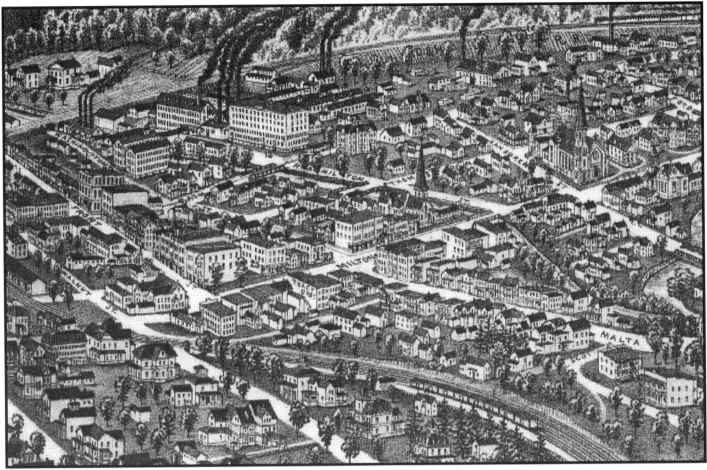

BALLSTON SPA
SHOWING THE VARIOUS PLACES THE MAN TRIED TO PASS THE BILL
DRAWN BY C. FAUSEL, TROY, N. Y.

door the man saw Morrison coming toward the stable. The man stepped into one of the stalls emerging moments later. At virtually the same time the boy returned to the livery with the note. Being a resourceful man Officer Morrison took the note from the boy before he could give the due bill back to the man. Morrison read the note then confronted the man with the evidence. Apparently the man was hungry as he immediately put the note in his mouth and chewed it to bits.

Morrison countered what he took as an insult by taking the man before the village police justice. Before the justice the man's explanation for his actions were simple, "My name is Billy Collamer (name #1) and I have a right to make as many notes in that name as I please; now what are you going to do about it?" Police Justice Smith had no trouble answering as he committed "Billy Collamer" to the village jail to await action by the grand jury.

The next day the stable boy went into the stall where the man had temporally disappeared to avoid Morrison. The lad found several sheets of paper that had been torn into shreds. One of the papers had writing on it. Putting the pieces next to each other he was able to find a second due bill. Like the one eaten by the man of many names, this one was signed by W. A. Collamer.

As the man lingered in jail awaiting trial other colorful tales from his illustrious career began to develop.

While the man was in jail he consented to be interviewed by a reporter from *The Ballston Journal*. In this interview he provided a rather vague account of his life. He would say he was born in New York state then refused to say where or give his name. He also refused to give his parents' names on the grounds that to do so would be to expose him to his parents' friends. He told the reporter that he worked on a farm until he was

83

eighteen years old, then in 1861 he joined the Union Army. He went on to say that he had been married for two years before he entered the Army and visited his wife while on leave. He told of how he had a fifteen-year-old son by this union. Again he refused to tell the reporter his wife or son's name or even where they lived. The man maintained that when his initial enlistment expired he re-enlisted and served an additional thirteen months. In the years following the Civil War a man who had reenlisted was a man to be respected. The man, never one to miss a point, said that in his second enlistment he had been captured and spent time in Libby Prison, the infamous Confederate prisoner of war facility. The man claimed to have been discharged in Jackson, Michigan. After the war the man claimed to have worked in various businesses but mostly in hotels "out west."

Throughout his confinement the man continued to refuse to give any of the various names under which he had lived. Although not admitting it was he, the man did acknowledge that many people felt his real name was Montague Flagg (name #2). Prior to the Civil War, Flagg, who was a native of the town of Malta, had worked in the Union Store in Ballston Spa. If Flagg and Collamer were the same man it would explain his reluctance to admit his real name. It seems Montague Flagg had had to leave town abruptly to avoid arrest for a felony. This was quite a different story than the man's claim that he had worked on a farm before joining the army.

While the man remained in the jail in Ballston Spa, a second set of allegations surfaced. Witnesses claimed the incarcerated man had been involved in a scam in Hadley, New York, earlier in the summer. Several people who had been in Hadley in June and who had seen the man in jail felt he was the same person who had pulled a successful swindle on Charles Rockwell. Rockwell was one of the leading citizen's of Hadley, who had lost a carriage in the transaction. The case was again a forgery similar to the one in Ballston Spa with two exceptions. The note passed in Ballston Spa had been only signed by one person. The two

in Hadley had been assigned to one person then signed over to one J. J. Draydon (name #3). In the Hadley scams there was a woman accomplice who went by the name of Maude Guernsey. At the same time that the sting was on for Rockwell, the man posing as Draydon was trying unsuccessfully to pass off a second note for $800.

It was assumed that Maude Guernsey was of a disreputable family from South Glens Falls (her brother had been convicted of burglary the fall session of the county court). Mrs. Guernsey visited the "man of many names" in the Ballston Spa jail several times, claiming to be his wife. To her he was known as John Moran (name # 4). Both Mrs. Guernsey and the "man of many names" admitted that they had a young son.

One of the more notable citizens raised in Ballston Spa was Judge D.W. Tallmadge, who was at the time serving in Brooklyn. Tallmadge wrote to the local newspaper that he was following the case of the man of many names and was sure that the man in custody was his former schoolmate, Mantaque Flagg. Tallmadge had been reintroduced to Flagg in 1872 when Flagg had pulled a petty scam on him in Brooklyn. It was probably a result of this loss that Tallmadge bothered to write the newspaper.

It was only natural that a man used to living by his wits would try at least one scam while in jail awaiting trial. This time the "man of many names" wrote a series of letters to the sheriff of LaSalle County, Illinois. In these letters, which were signed Patrick Lynch (name #5), the man claimed to have special knowledge of events concerning an unsolved murder that happened five years before in Norway, Illinois. In the letters, "Lynch" told of how two men had broken into the home of Petersen Kleppe, a wealthy farmer living just outside the village, hoping to rob him of what was rumored to be a large stash of cash secreted away in his house. Unknown to the robbers, Kleppe had a guest staying in the house, Benedick Sorensen. In a custom rarely practiced today, Kleppe and Sorensen were sharing a bed in one bedroom, while Kleppe's wife slept with the maid in the second bedroom.

The "man of many names" in his letters told of how the burglars were very clumsy and basically inept. They made so much noise as they entered through a window that they woke up both Kleppe and Sorensen. Startled, Kleppe had gone for the gun he kept loaded on the wall while Sorensen started wrestling with the intruders. In the onslaught that followed, Sorensen was shot three times, dying shortly after from his wounds. Kleppe was also shot once and the burglars thought he was also dead when they left the house. Fortunately, Kleppe had survived his wound.

"Lynch" told the sheriff that he knew these facts because at the time of the crime he was working as a sewing machine peddler in the area. "Lynch" reported that he met the burglars in a bar. Needing money he had agreed to drive them to Kleppe's and to wait for them while they pulled off the robbery. "Lynch" claimed he was paid $800 for his services.

So compelling and complete was "Lynch's" story that the sheriff of LaSalle County, along with one of his part-time deputies, came to Ballston Spa to interview the man going by the name of "Lynch." Luckily for history, the part-time deputy was also a reporter for one of the LaSalle county newspapers. When "Lynch" added that the names of the two men who committed the robbery were Lamb and Kenroy, the visiting sheriff believed his story in full. "Lynch" even added to his credibility by stating that Kenroy was in a Michigan prison serving time on unrelated charges. In following up on "Lynch's" story it was learned that in fact a man named Kenroy was in the Jackson, Michigan prison.

The case of a minor forger and con artist now took on an interstate political context that exceeded even the "man of many names" wildest

THE EAGLE HOTEL
STOOD AT THE CORNER OF MILTON AND BALLSTON AVE.
REPLACED BY THE POST OFFICE

expectations. The governor of Illinois wanted "Lynch" returned to his state to testify and resolve the Sorensen murder. The officials in Saratoga County did not believe "Lynch's" story. They argued that he should not be believed and wanted him to stand trial in this state. After the governor of New York was consulted, District Attorney Ormsby prevailed in having the man held for trial only. This decision had to have disappointed the deputy sheriff of Saratoga County. Since he had posted Lynch's letters he would have been eligible for part of the $1,700 reward in the Sorensen case.

Denied a trip to Illinois, the "man of many names," now calling himself Patrick Sullivan (name #6), tried to plea bargain with his those holding him. As "Sullivan" told it, he would rather spend a year in the workhouse (a minor level prison) than a year in the county jail. "Sullivan" would later say that this offer was not a confession, he only wanted a resolution.

"Sullivan/Flagg/Lynch's" trial added little to what was already known except that because he testified we know the "man of many names" alibi. "Lynch" told the court that on the Saturday evening, before his arrest, he was drinking in a tavern in Saratoga. He met a milk dealer from Malta that night who became his companion on a binge. Lynch said the man was short on cash and had offered Lynch the note for five dollars, saying he would pay Lynch back the entire note in Ballston Spa on Monday.

On his way to Ballston Spa on Monday, "Lynch" had started to question the honesty of the milk dealer (isn't there something about the pot calling the kettle black in that argument). After the milk dealer was not in the village, "Lynch" decided that he would probably never show. Since the dealer was not around "Lynch" had chosen to try to cash the note at the Eagle Hotel. Despite testimony to the contrary from several people involved, "Lynch" said he never tried to cash the note at any location except at the Eagle Hotel.

There were three milk dealers in the town of Malta. Each was brought into the courtroom. Each said that they had never seen the "man of many names" until the day they confronted him

in court. Their testimony failed to collaborate the alibi.

No one was surprised when the jury brought in a guilty verdict after deliberating for only ten minutes.

A couple of days later the sheriff transported the "man of many names" to Dannemora Prison. Along the way the man became very talkative. He admitted that his name was Mandeville Flagg. Flagg told the sheriff that he had concocted the story about Sorensen to avoid prosecution in Saratoga County. Flagg said told the sheriff that he knew the details because he had lived in LaSalle County while the case was unfolding and had followed the story in the local newspapers.

The people of Saratoga were relieved that for at least a brief period they would not have to deal with a man that changed his name more often than his clothes.

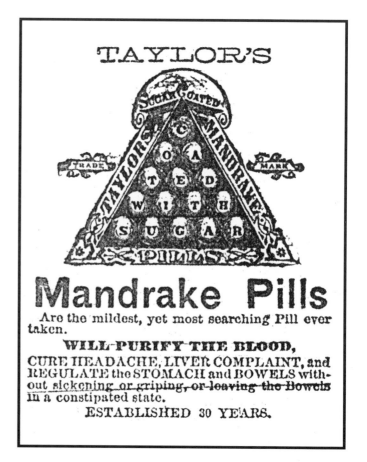

Too Many Barbers

Despite the cold and light snow there were people on the streets of Glens Falls on the evening of December 27, 1880. Several of those out that night noticed a man in a gray overcoat accented with a black collar, and wearing a derby style hat. The man was a stranger in the village who made an impression by skulking in the doorways that led to the second floor offices of the buildings on the west side of Glen Street. Over the course of a half an hour the unidentified stranger moved to different doorways up and down the street. Wherever he was seen he was consistently in a position to observe one specific small building on the east side of the street. At least one person that was out that night, one of the village's constables, thought he saw the man loading a pistol, but he did nothing about his observation.

A half-hour earlier at least two people, whose homes were on the southern end of nearby Bay Street, said they witnessed a man walking nervously for several minutes up and down the walk near their homes. The man they described matched the description that was used for the man lingering on Glen Street. It should be noted that the section of Bay Street where the man was walking was the neighborhood of the home of John Pair, a barber, whose shop the man appeared to be observing on Glen Street.

At almost exactly 9:00 p.m. the last customer of the day, Charles Cool, took a seat in John Pair's barber's chair. Cool had waited for two customers, but he felt it was worth it to get a professional shave. There were four chairs in the modest downtown shop but only two were in use this evening. As Pair began the shave, the other barber on duty, Charles Perry, began the functions required to close up the shop for the evening. Not being the owner, closing for Charles meant sweeping the floor for the last time and pulling the shades that covered the glass in the front door and windows. The only other window was in a side door of the shop. The side door was on the north side of the building (left as one faced it from the

street) and led into a long alley. There was a tall fence blocking the end of the alley that the side door exited into. The alley served primarily as a pathway to a privy at the back of the property. In the back of the building was storage of firewood needed to heat the small building, the privy and a community ash pile. Since the alley door was not used as a customer entrance there was no shade for the window - a simple curtain was used to give some privacy. The small building and its privy were the only structures that occupied the downtown lot. When Perry completed his mundane duties he left for the evening, walking home. Pair left Cool long enough to lock the front door behind his assistant, and then he resumed shaving his customer.

After Pair put a warm towel on his customer's face to soften his beard, he went behind the simple glass counter and picked up his daybook. Like Perry, Pair was trying to finish the tasks required for closing the shop so he could get home. He left the daybook on the counter so he could record his receipts as soon as he finished with Cool. Throughout the process of the shave Pair and Cool talked congenially. Cool would tell others later that Pair was in the best of spirits.

It was about 9:15 by the time the shave was finished. Pair unlatched the front door, letting Cool out onto Glen Street. After relocking the front door Pair returned to his daybook on the counter near the side door. Pair opened the cashbox and counted his receipts. After putting the cash in his pockets, Pair set about extinguishing the gas lamps. Before he could dowse the last lamp a shot rang out. The timing was so close to the closing that Cool, the last customer, had just reached the Presbyterian Church on Warren Street (a long block) when he heard the shot.

The bullet pierced the glass striking Pair first in the left arm. The power of the projectile was so great that it barely slowed as it went through his arm. The hot metal continued on its deadly mission shattering a rib, piercing both

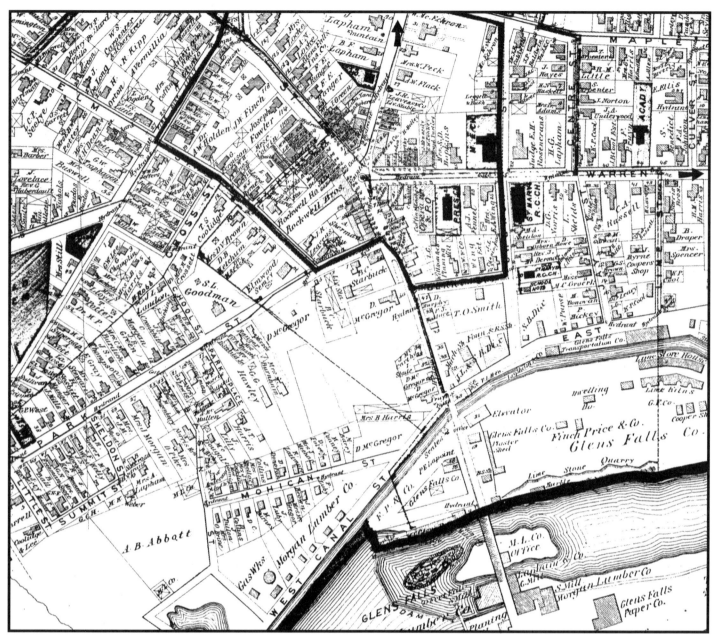

MAP OF GLENS FALLS
THE ASSAILANT WAS NOT FAMILIAR WITH THE AREA ESCAPING NORTH ON RIDGE STREET.
HE MEANT TO GO EAST ON WARREN STREET.
ATLAS OF WARREN COUNTY 1866

lungs, numerous veins and arteries before wedging in a rib on his right side. The force of the projectile hurled Pair backward onto the floor of his shop. He lay in the limited light gasping, for breath.

In 1880 there was only black gunpowder, which was loud, and smoked when fired. The assassin had stood so close to the door that the inside curtain was covered with the film of burnt powder.

Even though many of the other businesses

on Glen Street had closed at 9:00 there were still many people on the rapidly developing business end of Glens Falls at the time of the shot. Glen Street was redeveloping after a fire in 1876. This fire had burned much of the old downtown. Among the group on the street were those whose work required that they be out in that area at that time. This group included storeowners, employees of the stores and the teller of the bank (a position equivalent to manager today). The remaining people on Glen Street that night consisted of a

88

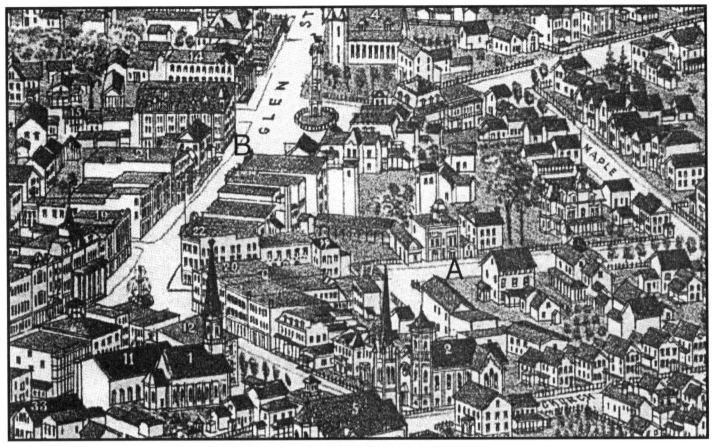

PANORAMA OF GLENS FALLS DONE IN 1888
A. THE FIRE HALL
B. THE SITE OF PAIR'S BARBER SHOP
PAIR'S BARBER SHOP HAD ALREADY BEEN REPLACED BY THE THREE-STORY BUILDING THAT STILL STANDS.
THE MAP SHOWS THE SHEDS FOR THE LUMBERYARD THAT HINDERED THE ASSAILANT'S ESCAPE.
THE BUILDING NEXT TO THE SHED IS THE FIRE HALL.
DRAWINGS BY L. R. BURLEIGH, TROY, N. Y. 1888

group of at least three men who had voluntarily congregated in the cold rather than go to their warm homes. Before the stores closed these men had been in a small group in the doorways that led to the upstairs offices. After the merchants had closed their businesses, these three men gathered in the large openings that served as entrances for the stores to avoid the light snow. The members of this group had all seen the man in the gray coat.

At the gun's report everyone out that night could tell that the sound had come from near the barbershop. Many of those in the area – if not most - hurried to the front door of the shop to see what had happened. From the entrance in front of the shop the men could hear deep desperate moans but because of the drawn curtains they were unable to see inside the building to determine the source. In seconds they moved like a swarm of bees to the side door where those near the front of the pack could see Pair lying on the floor in a pool of his own blood. Like the front door the side door was locked. Knowing of no other entrance the men broke a window to unlatch the door. Unfortunately for the investigation, the windowpane they broke was the same one through which the bullet had passed.

One of the first men in the shop bent down and felt Pair's pulse. Anticipating correctly that everyone wondered about his observations he declared to those who had gathered that Pair was alive but very weak. By the time the doctor arrived a few minutes later, Pair had taken his last breath.

The assailant knew, from being on the street himself, that there were people on Glen Street, so he made his escape through the alley. In order to get away he had to scale the fence at the back of the alley. His intent was to make it to Ridge Street where his presence in relation to the crime would be less noticed. Although he had surveyed his escape route, it was obvious he wasn't fully aware of all the obstacles. The route he chose went through an open section behind the Ridge Street Firehouse. The backyard of the firehouse abutted the property where the barbershop stood. He was forced to take this angular course because there was a lumberyard with a long shed that blocked a more direct route to Ridge Street. In the area behind the firehouse there was an overgrown pit that had been dug to be part of an icehouse. In the abandoned pit wild bushes had taken hold. Among the wild brush were burdock and cockle shrubs. In the black of the night as the man hurried through the yard the worst of any possible situation happened. One of the firemen had thrown out a pail of human excrement. In the dark the assassin stepped on the waste and fell into the pit. Desperate for the safety of the street, the man scrambled out of the hole. In less than a minute he reached the relative protection of Ridge Street. Some of the human waste was on his pants and burdocks and cockles were on his coat.

For a few minutes there was a belief that the shot might have been a suicide. However, the angle the bullet took when it penetrated Pair's arm and chest and the clearly visible footprints in the fresh snow immediately eliminated the possibility that the act was a suicide. No matter how obvious, a few people continued to believe the suicide theory for a few hours.

At the time of the murder Glens Falls was a large village. It was still small enough, however, that everyone felt that they knew everyone else's business. The validity of the reasoning then was as accurate as it is in similarly situated communities today. In the late 1900s the barbershop was one of the primary sources of local news, information and gossip. This was a time when to be clean-shaven meant one of two options. A man could do the equivalent of playing the lottery and use a straight razor on his own face, a proposition that on a good day would result in a few nicks and some missed section of whiskers. On a bad day shaving with a straight razor resulted in a person being an involuntary blood donor. A more appealing option was to go to a barber and get shaved, but that preference cost money. Since neither choice was totally desirable for men who labored in factories or other menial work, they often were only shaved once or twice a week. All professional men were shaved by a barber and usually had at the barbershop their own mug that was used to generate the lather. In Victorian America the visual indicators that a man was successful were: a new paper collar, clean cuffs, gold cufflinks, fancy shirt studs, a good suit freshly brushed and a clean shave. By middle age the requirements changed to include a slight paunch.

Men's facial hair changes in amount and form from generation to generation. There was a dramatic shift in the thirty years following the Civil War. During the war any man with a heavy enough beard wore one. By the turn of the century men were clean-shaven or at most had a mustache. Since it was foolish for a man to shave himself with a straight razor there was an increase in the number of barbers as the smooth face look came into style. Men used their trips to the barbershops as a time to get caught up on local gossip much the way women in small towns use trips to the beauty parlors today. Since the barber was the one who was the constant in the shop, he had the ability to guide the conversation. His opinion mattered and in political terms the barber's support was a necessary evil.

With Pair a barber, many men visited every week. Therefore, everyone knew, or at least thought they knew, his friends and enemies. What they did know is that John Pair thought himself the equivalent of the family's Horatio Alger's story (although the term would not come into play for several more years). He was a reasonably successful barber who had a continuous income. A regular income was something quite different from those who only worked as day workers or had seasonal positions. Pair had four children Jennie age fifteen, George and John both age fourteen and Eva age four. Pair was a widower.

Pair had trained two of his deceased wife's younger brothers, Edward and George Willett, to be barbers. He also provided them with a job and on many occasions a place to live. The Willett family had a relationship that made them involuntarily dependent on Pair. This dependency, and the fact that Pair had anglicized his name from the ancestral French spelling of Peare, caused some antagonism within the family. Immediately after the shooting four names surfaced as possible suspects. Among these names were Pair's two brothers-in-law, Edward and George Willett. The other persons who were considered suspect, included a neighbor in Glens Falls, Joseph Rehome, and John Mayo, a barber.

Initially the leading suspect was John Pair's brother-in-law Edward Willett. Edward became a suspect based on where he resided. In the back of Pair's barbershop was a small second room. Edward Willett, who was single, lodged in this one humble room. Edward, also a barber, was employed at Pair's shop. Although there were no known problems between Pair and Edward, the fact that Edward was absent at the time of the shooting made his candidacy as a suspect a given. Suspicions, limited as they may have been, concerning Edward's involvement were extinguished within an hour when he was found a few streets away in the company of a young lady named Lucretia Rehome. We know something of Edward's habits as those sent for him first checked the pool halls. At the time he was discovered Edward was being a gentleman and walking the young lady home. His alibi was complete when it was ascertained that the two had been seen among a group that had gathered at Pair's house for the whole evening.

Unlike Edward, his brother, George, was known to have had problems with Pair. His name, although known through the gossip that permeated the barbershop, was not taken seriously as George Willett was reported to have left for Chicago the previous September. The problem between Willett and Pair resulted from Willett's alleged intimate relationship with Pair's fifteen-year-old daughter Jennie, a minor who was seven

years his junior. The fact that the relationship linking George and his niece was legally forbidden added to the stress between the family members.

The third suspect was the first person who was considered really worth pursuing. As noted, John Pair lived on Glen Street near the intersection of Bay Street. Rumors among the neighbors and those at the shop had Pair engaged in a relationship with his neighbor Adeline Rehome. Adeline lived in what was called the Sisson House, which stood exactly on the northeast corner of Bay Street and Glen Street. Adeline was the mother of Lucretia, the young lady Edward Willett was walking home when he heard the news of the murder. The obstacle to Pair and Adeline's relationship was her husband, Joseph. As a potentially rejected husband, Joseph's name was bantered about seriously as a suspect for a several days.

When the police followed the tracks made by the assassin in the fresh snow they found that they led from the alley through the area behind the firehouse. They then went down an ally next to firehouse before exiting through a gate on the side. The tracks then led up Ridge Street in a northward direction. As the news of the murder spread through the community many people came out of their homes to see what had happened. Their tracks obliterated those of the assailant. With one left turn this northward route brought the assailant to the area of Pair's and Rehome's houses. It wasn't until Adeline confirmed that Joseph was home with her that evening from 8:30 on that Joseph was discontinued as a suspect. Because rumors about an adulterous relationship led to a possible motive, even when his wife told that he was home, Rehome remained a suspect in some people's minds for some time.

The most logical suspect to surface that night was the fourth man suggested, John Mayo. Mayo's name became known through discussions with Edward Willett, the resident of the extra room at the barbershop. It is worth of note that many who saw him that night were concerned about Edward's lack of feeling, as he stood calmly in the shop in the presence of the body of his employer/brother-in-law. In his calm voice Edward told the police that the day before Pair had foreclosed on a property in Fort Edward. The person displaced by the foreclosure was Mayo.

Prior to moving to Glens Falls the previous April, Pair had owned and operated a barbershop in Fort Edward for several years. To help with the cost of the move Pair put the shop on the market. At first George Willett managed the shop. This relationship ended when Pair found a letter from Willett addressed to his daughter. The letter was sexually explicit and considered to be disgusting. Pair confronted Willett and Willett wisely moved back with his parents who resided in Burlington, Vermont. Some time later Pair sold his business in Fort Edward to another barber, John Mayo. Over the course of the intervening months, while Mayo was running the old shop, he had fallen behind in his payments causing Pair to foreclose on the shop.

By the middle of the day following the shooting, it was learned that Mayo had moved to Fairhaven, Vermont. At first blush it appeared that the case of the murdered barber would have a quick resolution. A warrant was issued and officers were sent to Fairhaven to arrest Mayo. To be sure they brought back the right man the, officers took Edward Willett with them to Vermont. Edward spent the entire trip drunk.

The local newspapers were all following the case. Now, as in the Victorian Era, the motto *if it bleeds it leads* reigned supreme. Mayo's name was carried as the lead suspect by newspapers from as far away as Schenectady and Albany.

The officers brought Mayo back to Glens Falls where Warren County District Attorney Henry Howard interviewed him. Mayo had offered no resistance and in fact seemed to enjoy the excursion. For an alibi Mayo claimed that at the time of the murder he was giving a man a shave in Fairhaven. To add to his credibility one of the men who Mayo claimed was in the shop the night of the assassination was the local priest. When they wired Vermont the officers learned that Mayo's employer and others would come foreword to substantiate Mayo's whereabouts on the evening of the murder. Mayo, the man who would later add to his notoriety by publicly complimenting the sheriff of neighboring Washington County for having the best accommodations of any of his peers, was removed as a suspect and released from jail.

Within two days of his release in Warren County, Mayo notified the officials in Glens Falls that he expected to be reimbursed for the cost of his train ticket back to Fairhaven. Realizing that they were in a compromising position, the officials agreed to pay Mayo for his expenses. Mayo may not have been good at paying his bills, but it appears he was good at collecting what he was owed.

With Mayo eliminated as a suspect, rumors of who was involved exceeded solid suspects. Like in most situations of this type, where one incident dominates local interest, people tend to fall into one of four groups. 1. Those who saw something – relevant or not – these people try to build their small thread into the rope on which the solution to the investigation will hang. 2. There is also the group of individuals who saw something but do not want to get involved. 3. Individuals who saw nothing but talk as if they know all the relevant information in the case. 4. The group that consists of those people who just try to mind their own business. Judging by the problems they would have when they finally tried to find an impartial jury, we can assume this last group was very small.

Hearing about the unsolved murder on Glen Street many people suddenly felt that they had information relevant to what had had happened. Two of the people who came forward seemed to have some interesting, if not relevant, information. The first was Joseph Haviland who lived on a farm on Ridge Road two miles north of Glens Falls. Haviland had been out late the night of the murder visiting a friend. As he was unfastening his horse, he saw a man in the road in front of his property walking in a northerly direction. Like the man who had hidden in the doorways of Glen Street this man had on a gray overcoat and a black derby style hat. According to Haviland he would not be able to identify the man again because the man had pulled the collar of his coat up high on his face to protect himself from the cold. If Haviland was to be believed, the sheriff now had a direction that the man had taken in his escape.

The second person who experienced something peculiar that evening had much more to add to the investigation. Like Haviland, the widow Mrs. Sarah Wing also lived on Ridge Road north of Glens Falls. She lived on a farm with her son and brother. The Wing house was further out Ridge Road just north of a fork in the road. By 11:00 p.m. Mrs. Wing's brother and son had gone to bed. She was sitting alone when she heard a

knock on her door, which immediately attracted her attention. Instinctively she found herself looking through the window in the door. She was justifiably startled by the man's face looking back at her. The man had on a light colored overcoat and a derby style hat. Through the door the man asked for the quickest way to Sandy Hill (Hudson Falls). She started to give him directions through the door when he prevailed upon her to let him enter, adding that he would like a glass of water. Knowing that she could get help from her son and brother, Mrs. Wing opened the door and gave the man a much-needed drink of fresh spring water. As he drank from the ladle, Mrs. Wing provided the stranger with directions for the shortest route

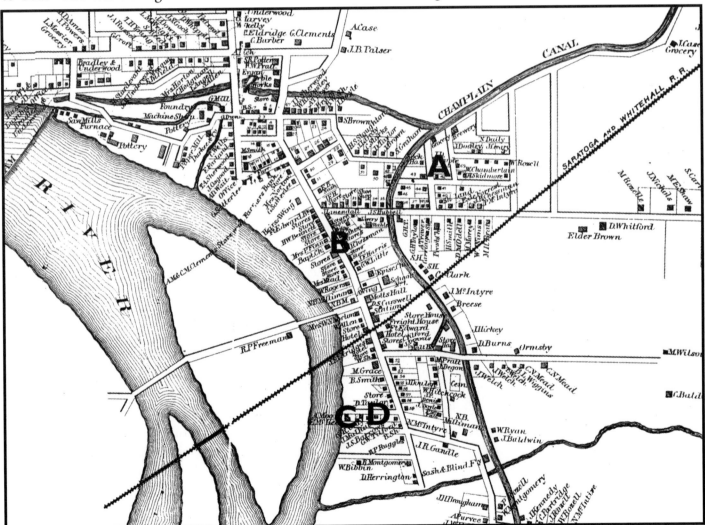

MAP OF FORT EDWARD
A. PAIR'S HOME
B. BARBER SHOP
C. PEARE'S
D. TERRAULT'S
ATLAS OF WASHINGTON COUNTY 1866

to Sandy Hill. The last Mrs. Wing saw of the man that night was as he was walking in the direction of the fork in the road.

Beyond the uniqueness of the situation several things about the nighttime stranger struck Mrs. Wing. First were his bright eyes. His slight French accent was a curiosity to her but not considered really unusual by Mrs. Wing since she was familiar with other people from Canada. The real curiosity that she could not get over was the fact that during their conversation the man said he was from Glens Falls, but did not realize that he was walking north instead of east in the direction of Sandy Hill. Mrs. Wing's memory of the stranger was locked in her mind when she realized that he did not have a horse but was walking at this late hour.

With Mayo eliminated as a suspect, another man virtually introduced himself as the principal suspect. George Willett, the brother of Edward, the man who slept in the back room of the barbershop, was unexpectedly at the wake held at Pair's house. At the outset, George Willett had been eliminated as a suspect because it was believed that he was living in Chicago. Suddenly and without explanation, Willett appeared in Glens Falls the night after the murder. The man trumped his own introduction as a suspect by selecting John Pair's wake as the venue at which to make his appearance.

There were two acts that added significantly to suspicions involving Willett. He was seen by several people in attendance that evening in what some felt was beyond a hug but would more accurately be described as an embrace of Jennie Pair. Jennie was the fifteen-year-old daughter of the deceased. Equally important, in the beliefs of the day, Willett was not seen looking at Pair's remains. To those engrossed in the Victorian values that dominated this period, a person needed a real reason not to look upon the body of a member of the family.

The Investigation

With Willett at the wake and not in Chicago the focus of the investigation now switched to him. After suffering the embarrassment of the highly publicized and too early arrest of Mayo, there were four questions that needed to be answered before the district attorney would have George Willett brought into custody. It was widely held that Willett had left for Chicago months before the murder. Had he actually gone there and if so when did he return to the area? If it could be shown that he was in the area at the time of the murder he would have opportunity, but would he have an alibi? Did he own clothes similar to the light gray overcoat and derby style hat that had been seen by many witnesses on the mystery man that night? It was understood that there was "bad blood" between the two men but was there a sufficient motive for Willett to want to kill Pair? The final question involved whether Willett had access to a weapon small enough to be carried under a coat yet powerful enough to do the damage that had been inflicted on Pair's chest.

Realizing the possible significance of his unanticipated presence on the scene, those investigating the murder immediately sought to determine where Willett was staying. It was soon learned that he was dwelling in Fort Edward at the home of his thirty-year-old sister, Alvina Terrault. Alvina was married to Mark Terrault who owned a business in Fort Edward where he painted carriages. The officers put the Terrault house under a loose surveillance while they also began interviewing some of the Terraults' neighbors.

The person who held the key to what appeared to be the main gate to the case was the Terrault's twenty-three-year-old neighbor Josephine Peare, referred to affectionately as Josie. Josie, her husband and their young daughter, Claudia, resided three houses away from the Terraults. More important than the proximity of her residence was the fact that Josie was on intimate terms with all the principals in the case. In addition to living near Alvina Terrault, Josie was also married to Wilson Peare, a cousin of John Pair. To the close-knit families of the area, Josephine was cousin and therefore someone to be trusted.

OLD FORT EDWARD
SHOWING SITE OF PEARE'S AND TERRAULT'S
BURLEIGH LITHO. CO. TROY, N. Y. 1894

For a brief period after John Pair's wife died and before she married Wilson Peare, Josie had moved into the widower Pair's house taking care of the four motherless children. Wilson Peare, Josie's husband, was also a barber with his own shop in Fort Edward, so through him she would also know additional tales about Willett. Since for several months George Willett had made a practice of always staying with his sister, Alvina, while he was in the area, Josie had a good idea of his comings and goings. If not the exact dates, at the very least Josie could provide the investigation with the relative times for any extended stays Willett may have had in the area. Through this one person the district attorney felt as if he had

discovered a gold mine of information. To add to her reliability there was not a history of disagreements between Josie and the Terraults. Even at this early period in highly publicized trials a defense attorney could capitalize on any animosity between a witness and the defendant to discredit the witness. This of concern on the part of Howard was predicated on the consideration that a defense attorney would ever be necessary.

Through Josie, the investigators were able to learn that Willett had arrived at his sister's sometime before 9:30 on the morning following the murder. As important as it was to place Willett in the region it was equally important to find out if he had an alibi for that evening, clothing similar to that worn by the suspect and access to the weapon. In the first meeting with the investigators Josie seemed to provide all the answers essentials to the investigation. To District Attorney Howard she appeared to be the lock that would seal the investigation.

Josie was able to collaborate that during the summer of 1880, after the Pair family moved to Glens Falls, Alvina Terrault became ill. With two sons, Artie, age ten and Eugene, age seven; Alvina needed help maintaining her household. She implored her former brother-in-law, John Pair to send his daughter Jennie to help manage the house. Jennie spent several weeks during July and August with her aunt. George Willett was living in the Terraults' house at the same time as this extended stay by Jennie. What Josie did not know was that sometime during the summer of 1880, Pair had found the letter and had become suspicious of the relationship between his former brother-in-law and his daughter. Against her will Pair had brought Jennie home to Glens Falls.

Josie was also able to add that the following September. She had been at the Terraults' for afternoon tea. At the same tea John Pair and Jennie had visited. As social events go this tea was amiable enough. After tea, Pair left Jennie in the care of her aunt and went out for a while with a man named King. Josie noted that almost immediately Jennie went upstairs alone. At about the same time Josie and Alvina went outside to play a game of croquet.

After a while, Jennie and Willett joined Josie and Alvina in the yard. Josie was surprised to see Willett. He had not been with the family at tea and Josie had not seen him since that summer when he had gone to stay with his parents in St. Albans, Vermont. She didn't know the details but she did know that Willett had taken his leave from Fort Edward at about the same time that Jennie had gone back to Glens Falls. There were two components adding to the intrigue of the "not too coincidental" meeting upstairs at the Terraults'. It was obvious that Willett had been upstairs the entire time the family was having tea. His election to stay upstairs begged the question

of, why had he not joined the group? Of equal importance was, why young Jennie had gone upstairs alone to meet her uncle? Since everyone was extended family, the potential of a rendezvous did not seem that apparent to Josie at the time. The meeting between Willett and Jennie should have been an issue to Alvina, since she was aware of Pair's suspicions about Jennie and Willett.

As the group sat on the lawn, Josie inquired as to why Willett had not come down to join the group. His response was brief but informative to the knowledgeable listener. "Because I don't want to see John," Willett continued, "You know I don't like John and he don't like me. And I don't care to meet him."

Charles Starks was the printer of the *Gazette* in Fort Edward. Starks was also a friend of the Terraults. Like Josie he had visited the Terraults' while Willett was there that day in September. Having been a regular customer of Pair's when he had the shop in Fort Edward and knowing that Willett worked in the shop, Starks asked if Willett was going to work for Pair in the shop in Glens Falls. Willett responded, "I wouldn't work for that __ __ son of a ____." As if name-calling was not adequate, Willett added, "I'll fix him before I die."

Adeline Terrault would later explain what happened the evening of the afternoon tea. She told how John Pair had reappeared in Fort Edward having found out that Willett had been hiding on the second floor. This time Pair had come to her house in search of Willett. Pair had not actually entered the Terraults' house but stood in the doorway while he asked Adeline the whereabouts of her brother. Adeline claimed that while he was in the doorway Pair had used inappropriate names for Willett. To get Pair out of her house, Adeline told Pair that Willett was with her husband in the carriage paint shop. Adeline would claim that her husband told her that when Pair got to the shop he had a pistol and threatened to shoot Willett. There is no record that Mark Terrault ever spoke publicly about the incident so we only have Adeline's word as to what occurred. Adeline also claimed that because of the language Pair used she

OLD FORT EDWARD
SHOWING THE SITE OF PAIR'S HOUSE AND SHOP
BURLEIGH LITHO. CO. TROY, N. Y. 1894

had banned him from her house. The excuse that Pair was forbidden to be at the Terraults' for bad language is rather weak, as Adeline appears to have been able to use as foul speech as anyone.

On the day following Pair's visit, where he supposedly had a gun, George Willett left the area for his uncle's home near Chicago. It would later be learned that Willett never worked the entire three months he was in Chicago. He stayed with his uncle and claimed that he was looking for work. However, Willett never brought any money into his uncle's home and was constantly asking his uncle for money to take mass transit in search of work.

The prosecution learned that what had started as a positive relationship between Willett and Pair had broken swiftly. Pair had trained George Willett to be a barber. For two years the two men had worked together in Pair's shop at 134 Broadway in Fort Edward. Willett even lived with Pair and his wife in their house. This was before Mrs. Pair's death. There had to have been some trust as Pair had Willett stay on and watch the shop in Fort Edward when he moved to Glens Falls. This was just before the take over of the shop in Fort Edward by John Mayo. The problem between the two men had to have happened during the summer of 1880 while Jennie was staying with her aunt. To the district attorney a motive for the murder seemed present but how sufficient it would be to a jury was still not clear.

As important as it was that Josie knew about the ill feelings between Pair and Willett prior to September, it was her presence in the Terrault house the morning after the murder that made her pivotal to the investigation. Through Josephine the investigators were able to piece together what happened and the parties' attitude in the Terrault house hours after the murder.

At 9:30 in the morning, under the pretense of needing some milk for her daughter, Josie went to see if Adeline knew of the shooting of Pair. For a little extra spending money the Terraults kept a dairy cow and Josie was one of their customers. The day after the shooting was one week after the winter solstice so it would not have gotten daylight until 7:30 in the morning. Josie's visit would have been considered relatively early in the morning. It was a cold December morning and the Terraults and Peares were close enough friends that Josie walked into the house without knocking. As Josie entered the house, Alvina was coming out of the bedroom. Alvina closed the door behind her. Closing a door was not something that would be commonly done on a December morning in the days before central heating since it would leave the room cold. The ever-inquisitive Josie immediately asked if Adeline had heard the news of what had happened to her former brother-in-law. At this time the two women only knew of the shooting, John Pair's condition was less certain.

"Have you heard the news?" asked Josie.

"Yes," replied Alvina calmly, assuming that the only real news was what had happened to Pair.

"Is it true?" inquired Josie.

Alvina took over the conversation, "Well Josie, if John is dead it is no better than he deserves." Her words exhibited the depth of the split within the family. Alvina continued her venomous words, "And for the old lady, [Pair's mother] I'm glad of it." Pair's mother lived with Pair and helped care for the motherless children.

Through her choice of words Alvina either inadvertently or deliberately went on to describe how deeply she despised John Pair. She told how Pair was "cross" and "ugly" to his family. Alvina would have known at least part of the story of what occurred in the Pair household as Jennie had lived with her twice that year. The first time Jennie was at the Terraults' for an extended stay was in the summer. There is a debate as to the reason for the second extended visit, which was in the fall and after the incident with Willett. Alvina would say that Jennie was kicked out of her home after John Pair learned of Jennie's determination to continue her relationship with her uncle. According to Alvina, Pair had banished Jennie saying, "I will not have any _____ living in my house." Needing a place to stay, Jennie, still a teenager, had moved in with her aunt. In contrast, Pair had told people in Glens Falls that Jennie was with her aunt because Alvina was still ill and needed support. Whichever story is true may never be certain, but we do know that Jennie lived with her aunt for ten weeks from the end of September until early December. Alvina took the problems of the morning as an opportunity to remind Josie that the death of Pair's wife, Alvina's sister, had been considered "queer."

Alvina talked of the destructive relationship between Pair and Willett, saying during the conversation, "John and George were never good friends." This was in direct conflict to the fact that Willett had lived with Pair for almost two years. She added that Pair had, "threatened to kill George." This comment was in reference to the time in September when Pair went to Fort Edward. Alvina went on, "We could have proved it and shut him up for it." So deep were Willett's feelings that he had allegedly told his sister "he would go to Chicago" and have Pair's "heart's blood even if it meant going to the gallows." Alvina reminded her neighbor that Willett was, after all, a "proud man." (A heart's blood was a term of the day referring to lifeblood.) The conversation that morning indicated that the Willett/Terrault family had discussed the situation between brother and brother-in-law at length.

At this point in the conversation the women saw a neighbor walking by the house. Josie, still wearing her coat, went out calling to the man to see if he knew if Pair was alive or dead. Alvina waited near the open door to hear the man's response. The women were told that the morning newspapers indicated that Pair was indeed dead. Emotionally moved by the news, Josie turned to Alvina and said, "let's go inside and talk about it." Alvina held the door as Josie walked back in the house. For some reason the door shut loudly. Alvina's action with the door may have been out of anger or inadvertent. In either event what happened as a result of the loud bang was momentous.

Suddenly from the bedroom came a call, "Alvina, Alvina?"

Josie was startled, assuming, up to that moment, that the two women were alone in the house. Josie looked questioningly at Alvina then asked whose voice it was. "George," responded Alvina.

Josie responded, "George is here? When did he come?"

Alvina told Josie that Willett had come that "morning" and was nearly frozen when he arrived. She said he was so cold that she had given up her warm bed so he would have a place to overcome his chill. (Keep in mind that according to Josie, Alvina was coming out of the bedroom when she went over at 9:30) The two women then went to the bedroom door, Alvina to check on her brother, Josie to give her greetings to the out of town guest. Alvina entered the bedroom first and told Willett to get back into bed and cover up so Josie could say hello.

What Josie caught sight of in the few minutes she was in the bedroom was crucial to the investigation. As soon as Alvina entered the room, she went to the far side and picked up a light gray overcoat that had been thrown carelessly over a chair. Alvina started to turn the coat inside out. As she held the coat Willett told her, "get it cleaned and fixed." He was obviously referring to the coat that Alvina was still holding in her hands. As if feeling an explanation was necessary for Josie, Willett turned and told her one of the buttons was off the coat. Even in the limited light of the room Josie was struck by his appearance. To Josie, Willett looked extremely pale. In her mind his whitish skin gave the impression he had just gotten over being seriously ill. Always curious, Josie asked about his health. Willett responded that he was not sick but rather he had just come from Chicago and was "all used up."

Josie asked when he had arrived. Willett and his sister replied in harmony "at half past two." The time was meant for in the morning.

According to Josie, Willett then reminded his sister for a second time that she needed to "get that coat cleaned."

The entire time Josie was in the bedroom Willett maintained his modesty by lying in the bed with his shirt still on. Josie noted that on another chair were Willett's pants and vest. They had been placed as if he had put them there in a hurry. On the bureau were his handkerchief, tie, collar and cuffs. It was what the items on the bureau were trying to cover that most interested the district attorney. It appeared to Josie that they were placed over a revolver. Her attention was caught by what she thought was a shiny band in the center of the pistol. She told the district attorney that the band appeared to be made of silver.

Josie wished Willett a belated "Merry Christmas" as she left the room.

At about the same time Josie left the bedroom the Terraults' young sons returned from the train station. They told their mother that their Uncle George's trunk had not arrived. Alvina explained to Josie that the boys had been sent to the station to see if the trunk arrived as it did not arrive with Willett. Stress of the day aside, Josie took her leave from the Terrault home at about 10:15, saying she needed to get back to her unat-tended daughter.

About eleven that same morning Josie returned to the Terraults'. This time Willett was in the living room with his sister when Josie arrived. He was wearing an undershirt and pants that had been stained by paint. Knowing that Alvina's husband, Mark, was a carriage painter Josie assumed the pants were his. Alvina and Willett told Josie that Willett's trunk had still not arrived. Josie assumed he had elected to wear his brother-in-law's clothes rather than his own, which were dirty from the trip. The dirt was the excrement thrown out by the fireman. To the district attorney, Josie added credibility to the completeness of her memory when she pointed out that Willett also had on his sister's slippers.

"Have you heard any more news?" all of them asked each other. It had only been an hour since Josie had left but they were all hungry for any tidbit of information.

Josie told them that she had heard nothing beyond the morning newspapers. She asked if they had read the various reports. Brother and sister exchanged glances before they answered in the affirmative. "Who could have done such a thing?" asked Josie.

"Well nobody knows," responded Willett as he paced slowly across the room.

Alvina picked up the gauntlet implied by the question adding, "Now Josie, you're part of the family and I'll tell you something which Ed [Willett] told me." She paused for a moment allowing the full impact of what she had to add build in intensity. "John was intimate with a married woman in Glens Falls." To add authority to her answer Alvina went on, "her husband was very jealous. He may have done it," she reasoned. The morning newspapers had said nothing of a jealous lover; the most they alluded to was the connection between Pair and Mayo.

Alvina's resolution to the issues seemed logical to Josie so she inquired as to Pair's children. Alvina answered, "Oh they're better off now. John whipped them a great deal." She let the impact of her comment settle then went on, "I don't believe they are sorry he is dead." The poison of her remarks then shifted to Pair's mother on whom she leveled this rather graphic retort. "I shouldn't care for the old woman if she lay in a gutter with her tongue hanging out of her throat."

A second point came out during this late morning conversation that both Adeline and Willett would later try to play down. According to Josie the three of them then talked about Pair's three thousand dollar life insurance policy. They all agreed that with the funds the children would all be provided for. The reason that Willett and Alvina Terrault would later play down the conversation is that knowledge of an insurance policy could contribute to the motive.

Willett showed he was already planning for the future adding, "We boys will run the shop, we'll advertise in Jennie's name and make slathers of money." By the boys he was referring to himself, his brother Edward and possibly Alvina's husband, Mark Terrault, who in addition to being a carriage painter had been a barber. It is doubtful he was including Josie's husband, Wilson, since he already had his own barbershop.

For a final time the three discussed how the morning newspapers were implying that the primary suspect was John Mayo. What they failed to say was that the source of the newspapers information was Edward Willett, Alvina and George's brother. Josie, Willett and Alvina all agreed that if the murderer were not Mayo it would most probably be the jealous husband. Before Josie left they all talked of taking the afternoon train to Glens Falls to attend Pair's wake.

At 11:30 as Josie was getting up to leave she said one more time, "Oh dear, who could have been so mean?" She paused in her thoughts for only a moment then added, "So low-lived as to do it?"

It was Willett who ultimately answered. His remark regarding whoever the assailant may have been was very telling, "Well, he's got his nerve." The implication was clear, even if obscure, that in Willett's mind it would take nerve to kill someone when they were totally not expecting an attack.

When Josie went to the Terrault house for the third time that day it was about 4:30 in the afternoon. Everyone seemed relieved that Willett's trunk had finally arrived. It would later be learned that the trunk had never been sent. Later that morning Willett had actually gone to the train station himself and wired the freight office in Albany to have the trunk sent.

While Josie was there Willett went into the trunk a couple of times to take things out that he needed for the evening. Each time he went to the trunk he used a key to open the padlock. When he obtained whatever he was after, he closed the padlock making sure it was fastened. The importance of his actions, as far as the distract attorney was concerned, was that they insured that whatever was in the trunk was there because Willett wanted it there and further he had knowledge of all the items present. With Willett keeping the trunk locked, he could not claim that someone planted items related to the murder.

Early in the afternoon Mark Terrault and his brother-in-law Peter Willett took a carriage to Glens Falls to supervise the funeral. Peter, who had come down for the funeral, was a barber in Burlington. Alvina stayed in Fort Edward to watch the children while George Willett and Josie Peare took the 5:45 train to Glens Falls to attend John Pair's wake. Josie was planning to ride the streetcar from the train terminal to the Pair home. Willett wanted to walk the relatively short distance. On the train to Glens Falls Willett told Josie to go ahead of him into the house, but not to tell anyone else he was there. He told her that he wanted to surprise Jennie. He did surprise Jennie as soon as he saw her, with a big and long kiss on the lips. To Josie this was an intimate act, far too personal to be performed in public. Alvina would endeavor to pass the same kiss off as social conduct common among French Canadian families.

Whatever the motivation, the act caused Josie's interest to peak. Having her own suspicions about the couple, Josie spent the rest of the evening monitoring their behavior. Keeping track of both of them at the same time turned out to be an easy task, since Willett never left Jennie side the entire time. He followed her around the whole evening like a puppy that suddenly found his master in the middle of a crowd. At one point Willett and Jennie dismissed themselves from the rest of those gathered to mourn and slipped into one of the bedrooms. Josie gave the couple a few minutes then walked into the room unannounced. She found the two sitting on a trunk with Jennie's head on Willett's shoulder. Willett had his arms around Jennie in what Josie considered an affectionate fashion. In Josie's opinion the embrace could not be classified as one of condolences.

Josie looked at the entwined couple and said, "Love in the dark."

"Who has a better right?" countered Willett.

"Go it while you're young." said the ancient twenty-three-year-old Josie.

Two days after the incidents at the wake Mayo was no longer a suspect. The interview with Josie made Willett the primary suspect in the eyes of those investigating the murder.

There are two very interesting and highly personal events that followed the wake. Rather than make the commute back and forth from Glens Falls to Fort Edward, the Willett and Terrault families literally moved temporarily into the Pair residence. The families stayed from the time of the wake until the internment. George Willett slept in John Pair's bed, a fact that made some people believe he was innocent. After all, how could anyone sleep in the bed of a person they had killed? It was extremely cold on the day of the funeral. When it came time to walk to the church and ride to the cemetery Willett realized he needed a scarf. He put on one of John Pair's and wore it to the funeral. The same group that thought sleeping in the bed was unbelievable thought the wearing of the person's clothes equally implausible.

One of the key issues was alibi. In 1880, long distance travel such as Willett's trip from Chicago to upstate New York meant the railroad. It didn't take long to learn that the reason Willett was constantly looking for his trunk. He had borrowed money from his uncle to take the train back to New York. Instead of paying the fare, Willett

had shipped the trunk while he had made the trip by whatever inexpensive method he could employ. For part of the trip he had ridden in boxcars, until thrown off the train by one of the guards they had working at each of the main shipping yards. Other times he posed as a passenger, until a conductor would throw him off the train for not having a ticket. Given his description and the route he took, his trek was easy to trace. Willett was not lucky when it came to the "bulls" who were paid by the railroads to throw vagrants from the trains. Over the course of his passage from Chicago to Fort Edward, no less than four security guards identified Willett as matching the description of a man they had removed from one of the various trains.

Even more supportive to the district attorney's case was that on the day of the murder several men claimed to have passed Willett as they walked on the railroad tracks between Fort Edward and Glens Falls. Each of the men who came forward to say they saw Willett on the tracks knew him personally. Unlike the railroad security that was using a description of Willett, the men on the track actually were sure it was Willett. Each of these men said they saw him early enough in the evening to give Willett plenty of time to be on Glen Street at the time of the murder.

Still other people came forward who claimed to have seen a man in a light overcoat walking the streets near the major corners in Glens Falls during the early evening of December 27th. One man went so far as to say he followed a man who had come out of the driveway adjacent to Pair's house in Glens Falls. The man fit Willett's description.

Josie's observations, in conjunction with the men on the tracks, was sufficient for the district attorney to consider seeking a warrant to question Willett, and search his belongings. Unfortunately for the district attorney an over anxious officer picked up Willett before he was ready to have him arrested. Part of the officer's motivation may have been a personal dispute between District Attorney Howard and himself.

The two men were "not much on speaking terms."

As has been mentioned previously in this book, police officers were allowed to share in rewards for the arrest and conviction of criminals. The murder of Pair was such an affront to the trustees of Glens Falls that they immediately offered a one thousand dollar reward for the person or persons responsible. At the time, Melville Bitley was an officer in Glens Falls. Bitley was one of the men who had been sent to Fairhaven, Vermont, to bring Mayo back for questioning. When Mayo was cleared Bitley immediately took an interest in those who were involved in the case. He watched the wake and the funeral that followed. He had seen George Willett and was aware that he was the prime suspect in the case. Pair's funeral began at the house; the people then went to a service at what was called the French Catholic Church on South Street. After the service the mourners went to the cemetery in Sandy Hill (Hudson Falls) for the interment. Bitley had followed the group the entire way. He waited in the warmth of the Washington Hotel until the funeral party left the cemetery. He followed them back to the Clark Hotel where he finally confronted Willett. To keep the shares of the reward to a minimum, Bitley brought Willett back to his son's hotel where the Bitley family housed him for several days. Willett offered no resistance and was not shackled in any way.

Late in the day of the funeral Bitley brought Willett to Howard's office for questioning. Howard had Pinkerton Detective Hotchkiss with him while he questioned Willett. Even at this time any statement a person gave after they were arrested and before an attorney was called could not be used later in court. The absence of a lawyer at the questioning would play heavily in the legal hassle that was to follow. During the interview in Howard's office Willett made several comments that contradicted each other. At one point he said he got to Fort Edward on a passenger train then later said he had jumped a freight train. He also gave different accounts of what he did during the time he claimed he was in Albany. To Howard, these contradictory statements amounted to a confession.

There was one other comment made by Willett that the prosecution felt summed up its case. While Willett was Howard's office he had taken off his outer coat, hat and scarf. As potential witnesses were brought in to see if they could identify Willett as the man on the street before the murder they asked him to put on the outerwear. When he came to the scarf Willett allegedly said, "That's not the scarf I had on that night. That's Pair's scarf." To two of the witnesses present when the comment was made this was equivalent to a confession.

With a proper warrant the Pinkerton agent and a local officer went to get Willett's trunk. In addition to personal items and clothing, the trunk, which was still padlocked, yielded a small caliber pistol and two pocketknives. Willett's coat yielded a second small caliber pistol, more knives and a little over $2.00 in change. In the trunk was a box containing 32-caliber cartridges. These shells were too big for either of the two pistols that had been found. The Pinkerton agent asked Willett why he had the oversized shells. Willett told them that there was another gun hidden at the Terraults' home. Willett said he had hidden it because he was afraid that Adeline's sons might find it and play with the dangerous weapon. Willett had done nothing equivalent to hide the two pistols that were in his possession.

The missing gun turned out to be the one Josie saw on the bureau and believed was a revolver. In fact it was what was referred to as a pocket rifle. This gun was found on the top self in the pantry of the Terraults' home, behind some chinaware.

A detective from the Pinkerton Agency took the coat into his possession. The outside of the coat had been cleaned. However, in looking closely the detective could see that part of the lining of the coat was covered with burdocks and cockles. The coat was identified as the same one that Willett was seen wearing when he visited Fort Edward the previous September.

The pocket rifle was an interesting discovery. Wesson Firearms manufactured the gun

THE CLARK HOTEL
SITE OF WILLET'S ARREST
BUILDING IS ACROSS THE STREET FORM FORMER
WASHINGTON COUNTY COURTHOUSE IN HUDSON FALLS

before the company merged with Smith to become Smith and Wesson. The pocket rifle fired a 32-caliber cartridge. This size cartridge was most commonly used in a pistol. The pocket rifle, however, had a seventeen-inch barrel much longer than the five-inch barrel associated with pistols of the period. Since the speed of a bullet increases as long as it is in the barrel of the gun this addition-al length provided additional rifling and propul-sion. When one compared the same size shell fired from a pistol to the pocket rifle it was obvi-ous that the pocket rifle had much more stopping power. What was most incriminating was that the Wesson gun was one of the very few ever manu-factured in America where the barrel created a left hand rotation. The marks of a counterclockwise action were found on the bullet that killed John Pair.

The trunk produced other elements important to the case. In the trunk, banded together, was a collection of letters from Jennie to Willett. These letters were written over the course of the summer of 1880 until November of 1880. In the trial that would follow there was public embarrassment for many women in attendance, as the letters demonstrated that the relationship between uncle and niece was physically intimate.

Two of the letters give a timetable for September 1880 and provide some indication of how the various family members regarded the relationship between Jennie and Willett. On September 22, 1880, Jennie wrote a letter to Willett in Chicago, postmarked from Glens Falls. The letter of the 22nd was very intimate and revealed that their relationship had become physical. The contents of the letter were considered too shocking for Victorian Society so the exact contents have been lost to history, but the perception of what was said was recorded. It was said that women of good character would leave the room rather than hear the contents of the letter. There was a second letter dated September 29, 1880. This letter was postmarked from Fort Edward. In this letter Jennie explained that she had been sent by her father to live with her Aunt Adeline. She took the opportunity to tell Willett that her banishment from her father's home was good because she would no longer have to "steal away from home to see" him. Obviously, Jennie felt that Adeline did not object to the relationship. This might explain why Adeline said nothing when Jennie went upstairs after the tea. There was a letter written in mid-October that expressed affection but little else. It was the last letter in October that showed that Jennie was becoming troubled by Willett's behavior. In the letter Jennie admonished Willett for having written to her father. She said the following, "You were very foolish to write to him. I would not have satisfied him enough to write to him, if I had been you." Jennie went on to say that her father had not written to her lately.

The letter written by Willett to Pair was never published but Willett did save Pair's response to him. On October 21, 1880, Pair wrote:

"I have no favors to grant you. You have done everything bad that a man could do to another and you ask for some favors. You have broken up my home. You have destroyed my daughter: I have this to say that whatever bargain you make with her I find no fault. She's not under my care no more. The only thing I have to say is this. If Jennie should come to the worse and throw herself away to bad the only thing that will settle this is your heart blood if I ever come across you. But if you should marry her then the thing would be settled."

It is obvious that Willett had requested something of Pair but exactly what is not clear. It doesn't appear that the request was for Jennie's hand, as Pair says in the letter that he would have agreed to a marriage. So what could the request have been that Pair was willing to respond, even if he did reject it?

The last letter from Jennie to Willett, that was written that October, provides one possible answer. In this letter Jennie told Willett that she was becoming concerned about one of his fixations - her father's barbershop. The following is part of the letter:

"George you are commencing again about the shop. George I cannot stand that. You must give up that object. Don't think of him. You are all right. You are out of the reach of him so don't trouble yourself. George you will get me crazy if you commence about that again. Let things go as they will,"

Jennie was also becoming concerned about the way Willett expressed his love for her. It appears from the paragraph below that Willett was becoming jealous or at the very least threatening to leave her.

"George I think that you use very funny language towards someone that you claim to love so well. I don't think that when you say 'if you mention this to anyone that will be the last.' I don't think that proves that you love me."

In late November Jennie wrote to George telling him that her father had written to her asking her to come home. For whatever reasons Jennie had changed her mind about not returning, and was considering going back to her father's home in Glens Falls. She asked Willett to continue writing to her at Adeline's house. Three weeks before the murder Jennie returned to her father's home on Glen Street in Glens Falls.

Adeline would later tell that upon hearing the news that Jennie had returned to her father's house, Willett wrote one last letter. The letter, which was lost, was not received until after Jennie had returned to Glens Falls. Upon hearing there was a letter for her, Jennie went to Fort Edward to visit her aunt and more importantly to read the letter from Willett. In the note, which Jennie read out loud to her aunt, Willett told his young mistress that based on her decision to return to her father's home he would no longer write to her.

From these letters the investigators felt that they could prove a motive and maybe even two. One motive would be Willett's desire to be with Jennie, the weakness of this motive was John Pair had said in writing that he would give his blessing to a marriage. The second motive was how Willett seemed to be obsessed with a desire to own the barbershop. The letter from Jennie, in conjunction with the testimony of Josie Peare where she said Willett had said that "the boys" would operate the shop, seemed to indicate that ownership of the business was a motive. Later the district attorney would add the insurance policy as a financial incentive.

In March of 1881, the case was taken before the grand jury. After hearing the evidence presented by Howard, Willett was charged with first-degree murder. Willett was held in the Warren County jail in Caldwell without bail until his trial began the following September.

The Trial

Although unable to pay for his own lawyer, Willett could not have had a better defense attorney. At the time of this trial there was one defense attorney in the area whose skills before a jury exceeded every other lawyer. His name was Charles Hughes. This was not the Charles Hughes who would go on to be on the United States Supreme Court but rather a more modest gentleman from Sandy Hill. This Charles Hughes had been involved in virtually all the major cases in the area for the preceding decade. In 1871, Hughes had been called in after Charles Shaw, of Cambridge, New York, had been convicted in the

FORMER WARREN COUNTY COURTHOUSE
THE SCENE OF WILLET'S TRIAL
LAKE GEORGE HISTORICAL ASSOCIATION

CHARLES HUGHES
ATTORNEY FOR THE POOR
PICTURE COURTESY OF THE WASHINGTON
COUNTY ARCHIVES

daughter was murdered in the early 1880s. One of the local doctors was charged with prescribing an excessive amount of poison.)

On the opposite end of the social spectrum was the 1878 trial of Jesse Billings. Hughes defended the extremely wealthy Jesse Billings when he was charged with the murder of his wife. In the Billings case, like in the Shaw case there were two trials. The first trial ended in a hung jury (the jury stood eleven to one for not guilty). At the second trial Billings was found not guilty. Of the twenty-four jurors that heard the evidence twenty-three thought it insufficient to convict Billings.

Obviously, a man of Hughes' skill did not come cheap. Although it is not clear exactly where Hughes' fee came from, George Willett's brother Jacob, who lived in Vermont, paid a portion of the bill. Jacob mortgaged his farm to help his brother. There was one other brother, Octava, who lived on Glen Street in Glens Falls. The care of Pair's children was given to Octava.

When he went into a courtroom Hughes had two things going for him. First, he was, by his very appearance, intimidating. He was tall, had a long beard, and a glare that could put anyone in their place. When in court he tempered his appearance with a soft voice. His greatest skill, and the one that people went into the courtroom to see, was his ability to anger the opposing counsel. In the Billings case Nathan Moak, the prosecutor from Albany County, had been brought in to help. Hughes made Moak so angry that at one point he literally stood in the courtroom and screamed for justice.

In contrast to Hughes' experience and temperament of Hughes was Warren County District Attorney Henry A. Howard who headed the prosecution. When it came time for Willett's trial, Howard, who was only thirty-five, understood what, or maybe better stated, whom he was up against. To help with this important case, Howard brought in John Hill of New York City to help in the prosecution.

By the time the trial began on September 19, 1881, the press had managed to build up the

murder of his wife and three of his daughters. Hughes was able to have his execution postponed and a retrial ordered. In the retrial Hughes cast enough reasonable doubt stating the real cause may have been attempted suicide on the part of the wife that Shaw was allowed to go back into society. (One of the most disturbing parts of the Shaw case occurred years later at the same time the Willett investigation was going on. A fourth Shaw community's interest in a drama between the lawyers. The stage was set for an exhibition in the courtroom rarely seen in this part of the state. In the county seat of Caldwell, there were two adversaries ready to seek victory, if not justice. The amount of newspaper coverage in the case prior to the trial was so great that it took a day and a half just to select a jury that was believed to be nonbiased. It was, at this same time, common to have an entire murder trial take less than a day.

With no eyewitnesses to the crime, both sets of advocates knew that the case rested on how the jurors weighed the circumstantial evidence and these men's (juries were all men) opinions about the honesty of the witnesses. Although the task would be much easier for the prosecution, the lawyers for both sides felt that they would be able to explain the circumstantial aspects of the case. If the attorneys were correct that they could explain the evidence, then the sense of sincerity projected by each witness would be the critical turning point.

As the pretrial revelry was warming up, it was recognized through the newspaper coverage that an unusual event was going to happen. This trial would most assuredly rest on the testimony of women. Everyone interested in the case had heard of the opposing witnesses, Josie Peare and Adeline Terrault. It was widely speculated that Pair's alleged mistress, Mrs. Rehome, would also appear. On the spicy side, the people in the county were anticipating that Jennie Pair, a girl so intriguing that a man would kill her father to be with her, would be placed on the stand.

As the trial opened one of Hughes' first requests was for funds to bring many of his witnesses from Fort Edward to Caldwell. Hughes explained that the people involved were poor, but

THE WARREN COUNTY COURTROOM
MAINTAINED MUCH AS IT WAS AT THE TIME OF WILLETT'S TRIALS.
LAKE GEORGE HISTORICAL ASSOCIATION

that to have a fair trial he needed them present to support his client. One must be mindful that the judge would have to know that District Attorney Hill's expenses were already being borne by the county. Hughes' request for expenses was granted and thus began a very expensive trial. This trial would be so expensive that it would strain the pockets of the people of Warren County to the level that, at one point, there would be a discussion of floating bonds to temporarily offset the need for revenue.

The prosecution tried to make the case seem straightforward. Howard and Hill laid out the evening of the murder and the reason why Willett had become a suspect. The prosecution wanted to be sure all the other suspects were explained away so they actually brought Mayo back from Fairhaven to testify to his alibi. They put Mrs. Rehome on the stand to explain where her husband was on the evening in question. It should be noted that during her testimony Mrs. Rehome was one of the people who reported seeing the mystery man on Bay Street half an hour before the murder. There were two other points that were not evident until the trial. The prosecution would hold that it was Willett's intention to make it to Fort Edward by 11:00 p.m. in order to take the train back to Albany. One of the few new arguments that would come up during the trial had to do with the amount of money found on Willett. The prosecution would attempt to use the fact that he almost exactly enough money to pay for a trip to Albany then return the next morning. If he had made that train he would have arrived in the morning with his luggage and no one would have suspected him. They made a strong point of his mistake of going out (north on) Ridge Street instead of taking Warren Street (east). According to the prosecution it was the confusion of the streets of Glens Falls that had made Willett's plan go astray.

In addition to Josie's testimony the prosecution would try to establish opportunity by bringing in men who had thrown Willett from the train and a series of men who all knew Willett, and said they saw him late in the afternoon of the murder, walking toward Glens Falls.

Cases based on circumstantial evidence need to clearly establish motive and opportunity, without creating a feeling that there was animosity of a witness toward the defendant. Josie Peare's testimony was essential for both motive and opportunity. With so much resting on this one person's statements, the prosecution also sought to show that Josie had nothing to gain by her being on the stand. Howard and Hill both knew that Hughes was a master at placing doubt on the credibility of a witness. To remove any trump card that Hughes may have on Josie, the prosecution tried to eliminate the issue of animosity by establishing that Josie had no issues with either the Terraults or Willett.

Josie proved to be every bit the witness the prosecution had hoped for. She appeared sincere, took no time in answering questions, and most important, did not seem to bear a grudge toward Willett. If Josie were believed by the jury, opportunity was established as well as motive. Josie was the person who found Willett and Jennie sitting on the trunk in the bedroom. Josie was in the Terraults' house when Willett had been hiding upstairs. And most important Josie had seen Willett's gun the day after the murder in his sister's bedroom.

For the prosecution, the remainder of the motive was found in Jennie's handwritten notes to Willett. It was unambiguous from the letters that uncle and niece were physically intimate. The letters also made it clear that Pair knew of the association, and had acted to end the relationship. Willett's flight to Chicago added credence to the motive, since it indicated that he was in all probability afraid of Pair.

The defense's case would focus on trying to establish that Willett was not in the area. If they could get the jury to believe he was in Albany, he would not have had the opportunity. Without opportunity, there was no case. The problem was that one of the primary witnesses called by Hughes didn't project credibility. That man was the owner of a diner near the Albany train station. The defense wanted the jury to believe that Willett had spent the evening in the diner.

THE CHURCH CONSTRUCTED BY WILLETT
DISPLAYED AT FORMER COURTHOUSE
COURTESY LAKE GEORGE HISTORICAL ASSOCIATION

Unfortunately, the man's establishment was rather better known for satisfying other appetites besides hunger, so he was of little help, and in all probability, took away from the defense.

The defense also tried to establish that there was really no motive. The strongest argument was the last sentence in the letter from Pair to Willett, written while Willett was in Chicago. Pair had written, "But if you should marry her then the thing would be settled." Hughes tried to argue that to believe the prosecution's theory regarding a motive, that Willett took Pair's life to be with Jennie, was ridiculous, as Pair had already given his blessing to a union.

Adeline Terrault was the principle witness for the defense. To detract from the argument of opportunity, she would continually hold that her brother had not arrived until the morning after the murder. To try to remove some of the pressure regarding motive she would hold that the negative relationship between Pair and Willett was all Pair's doing. Hughes was not able to explain why the jurors should hold much stock in a woman who had arranged for her under-aged niece to be physically involved with her adult brother.

Adeline also had a lot of trouble under cross-examination, which was led by Hill. Except for what happened the day after the murder, Adeline couldn't remember many details in her life. She expected the jury to accept all the minute details of that one day, yet could not remember the year she was born, her children's ages, or the year she was married.

The jury had two distinct choices. They could either believe Adeline or they could believe Josie. There was no way they could believe both. Josie had shined on the stand as compared to Adeline.

Expert witnesses were still a relatively new phenomenon in America's courts as was forensic science. Because they were new and not exact, experts were often not taken too seriously. In this case both sides would attempt to advance their case by utilizing expert testimony involving the gun. By the time the trial was well underway it was recognized that the weapon used to kill Pair

was either the pocket rifle, found in the Terraults' pantry, or a gun of the same make. This conclusion came because of the unique left hand rifling of the projectile. It is interesting that the weapons expert used by the prosecution, Charles Leet, came from Connecticut and was the same man used in the Billing trial a few years earlier. The choice of Leet may have been an unwise choice as Hughes had experience dealing with Leet's testimony. Leet was born in Austria and spoke with a heavy accent, a second fact that would not bode well with the farmers on the jury, who would consider themselves true Americans. Perhaps the most damaging part was the fee Leet's charged. He was paid $150 a week to serve as an expert witness. At this time a farmer or factory worker was living on about a dollar a day. In contrast, Hughes, a man always able to see the political ramification of a witness, used M. I. Buswell, a gunsmith from Glens Falls as his expert. He was in all probability a man known to some of the jurors. Jurors many have even used Buswell to

THE CELLS DOORS OF THE WARREN JAIL
IN THE BASEMENT OF THE FORMER
COUNTY COURTHOUSE

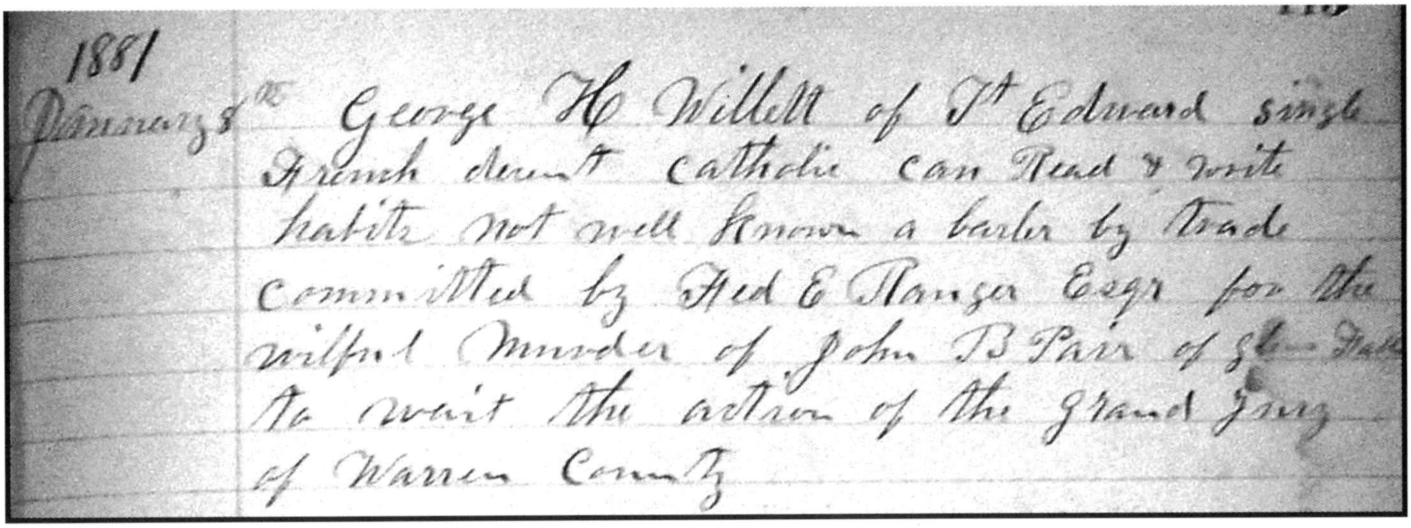

1881

[handwritten jail record entry]

JANUARY 8TH GEORGE WILLETTT OF FORT EDWARD, SINGLE OF FRENCH DESCENT, CATHOLIC CAN READ AND WRITE, HABITS NOT WELL KNOWN, A BARBER BY TRADE, COMMITTED BY FRED E. RANGER ESQUIRE FOR THE WILLFUL MURDER OF JOHN PAIR, TO AWAIT THE ACTION OF THE GRAND JURY OF WARREN COUNTY

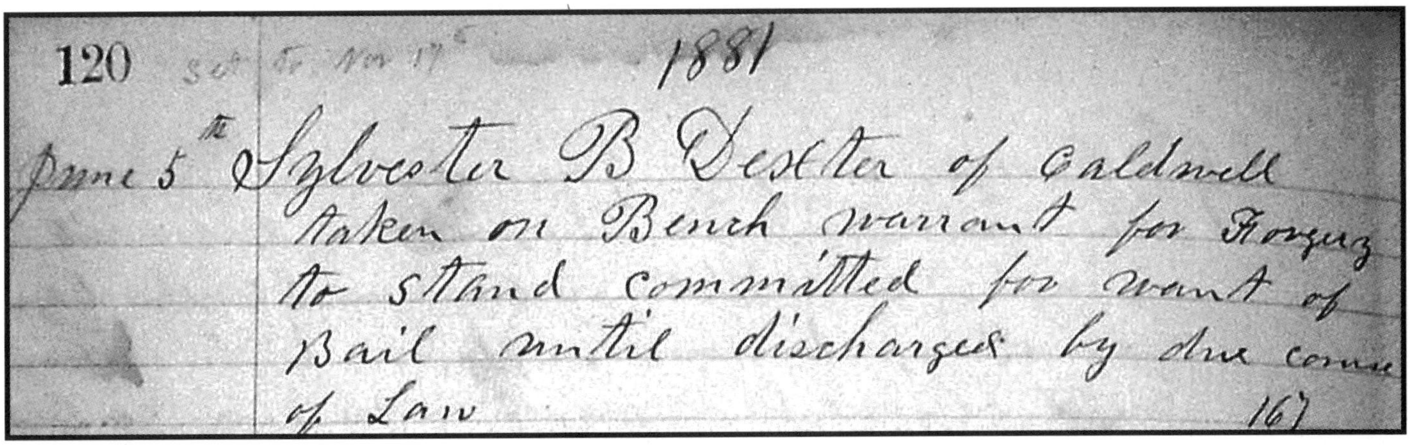

120   *1881*

[handwritten jail record entry]

JUNE 5TH SYLVESTER B. DEXTER OF CALDWELL TAKEN ON BENCH WARRANT FOR FORGERY TO STAND COMMITTED FOR WANT OF BAIL UNTIL DISCHARGED BY A COURT OF LAW.
NOVEMBER 19TH GAVE BAIL COURT OF SUPREME

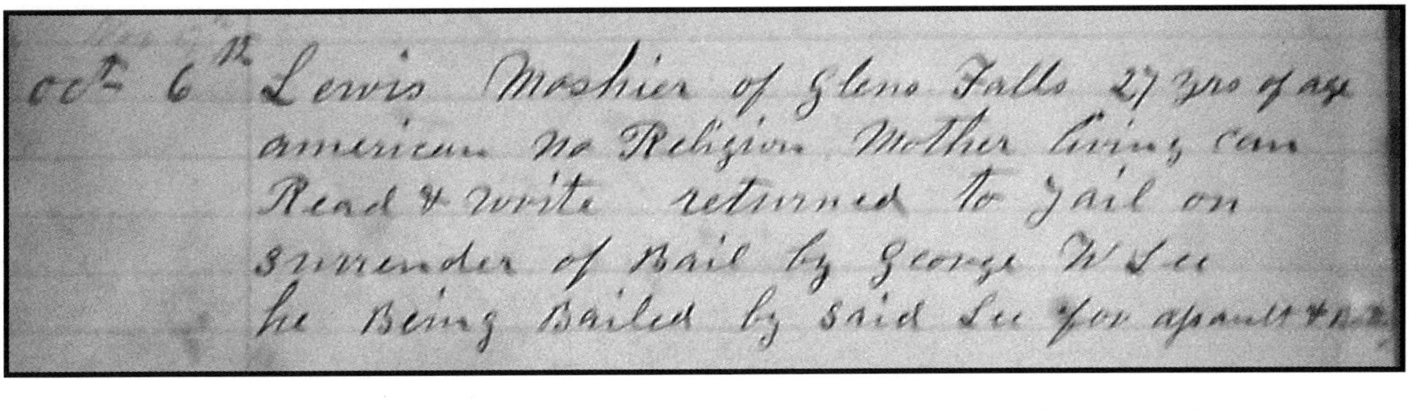

[handwritten jail record entry]

OCT. 6TH LEWIS MOSHIER OF GLENS FALLS 27 YEARS OF AGE AMERICAN NO RELIGION, MOTHER LIVING, CAN READ & WRITE, RETURNED TO JAIL ON SURRENDER OF BAIL BY GEORGE WHITE
HE BEING BAILED BY SAID __ FOR ASSAULT & BATTERY

repair their own guns.

The only truly creative event that took place in the court was the defense's trying to confuse the ownership of the gray coat overcoat. The confusion included how the burdocks got on the coat. Hughes consistently tried to show that Willett did not own the coat until he got to Chicago. The prosecution placed several witnesses on the stand who tried to show he owned the same coat before he left for Chicago. The importance is that the witnesses who said he had the coat in September were the same people who testified to comments made by Willett about Pair. The importance of this distinction is limited, since in either case he did own the coat. The defense tried to show he bought it in Chicago in order to discredit the witness who said he had the coat in September.

It was the explanation of the burdocks that was far more creative. Hughes put the Terraults' handyman on the stand to say that in the two days that Willett stayed at the Terraults' he (the handyman) had warn the coat to do his chores, which included milking the cow. Remember, Josie had gone to the Terraults' that morning to get milk for her daughter. On one occasion the handyman had fallen into a burdock bush, so he was the reason for the burdocks being on the coat.

Everyone who came to the courtroom as the trial ended was disappointed that Jennie Pair was not called to the stand. She was in attendance in the courtroom almost every day of the trial, but was never called to testify. In all fairness there was little that she could have added to the facts. She was not with Willett at the time of the shooting so she could not have relieved the issue of opportunity. Her letters were already in evidence so she would have been hard pressed to dispel the possibility of love as a motive. What she would have contributed was some real racy color to the proceedings.

The jury started their deliberations on Saturday at 8:00 p.m. They were only out for six hours. At two in the morning the jury bell rang. The verdict was predictable, and it would have been difficult to find anyone who would have bet

against the guilty verdict from the jury. George Willett was sentenced to be hanged on December 2, 1881, a little less than a year after Pair's murder.

The Appeal

With only two months between the end of the trial and the execution, shortly after the conviction Hughes filed a petition for a retrial. Pending a resolution on the question of the retrial, Hughes asked for an extension of the date of the execution. In late November, Judge Landon heard Hughes' arguments regarding both an extension and a retrial. In his typical manner, Hughes argued his points for over three hours. Hughes' primary issue was that the judge had allowed the testimony of the Pinkerton detective. Even at this time what a person said after being arrested could not be used against them, if they had not had the opportunity to have an attorney present. The prosecution, represented again by John Hill, took less than forty-five minutes to put

WILLETT'S CELL FOR THREE YEARS
BASEMENT OF FORMER WARREN
COUNTY COURTHOUSE
LAKE GEORGE HISTORICAL ASSOCIATION

forward their points. The judge promised an answer on Thanksgiving Day.

Escape

Willett proved to be a man who would resist, at all cost, the ability of others to control his destiny. The Tuesday before Thanksgiving, while Judge Landon was reviewing Willett's legal options, a story broke that Willett had tried to set up an escape from the Washington County Jail. According to the reports, while Willett was incarcerated he had befriended fellow prisoner Louis Mosher. It was expected that Mosher would be released in early November. Originally, Willett was going to have Mosher smuggle out a letter to be given to his brother Edward. When it became apparent that Mosher was not going to be released, Willett turned to a second prisoner, Sylvester Dexter to serve as the courier. At the time Dexter was being held on a minor charge of forgery. Knowing that Willett's letter could be used to his advantage, Dexter set about negotiating with the sheriff. The deal that resulted provided that if Dexter could obtain a letter from Willett, which he would then turn over to the authorities, the forgery charges would be dropped. Assuming Dexter was leaving the jail, Willett provided him with the letter to his brother Edward. Dexter did leave but not under the conditions that Willett expected. Willett had no way of knowing it, but the newspapers carried the story the next day.

The week after Thanksgiving and days after the public knew of Willett's escape plans, Hughes met with his client. Hughes asked Willett if he was planning an escape. Willett, unaware that the letter had been turned over to the sheriff, assured his attorney that he had no such plans. Hughes then showed Willett the letter that had been provided by the sheriff. Willett admitted writing the letter but denied that he had actually planned the escape. Hughes reprimanded Willett, saying that if there were any further attempts at

CELL WINDOWS
THROUGH WHICH PEOPLE WOULD VISIT WITH WILLETT
FORMER WARREN COUNTY COURTHOUSE LAKE GEORGE

self-liberation he would "abort all efforts" on his behalf. Hughes then told Willett the relative good news that the judge had ruled that he would have the case reviewed in the January term.

The letter proved to be an embarrassment for Willett on many levels. The newspapers characterized the letter as an example of bad spelling. All the letters found in Willett's trunk were those he received not those he had mailed. This was the first time the reports showed Willett's writing ability. The plan that he outlined was so simple and audacious that it may have worked. He asked his brother Edward to enlist the support of two other men. He suggested that Dexter might be interested in being one of the men. Then Edward and one of the men would pose as deputy sheriffs from another county. The third man would play the part of the prisoner. They would ask the sheriff if he would hold the man overnight. When the Sheriff had the keys out they would pull their guns and shoot as necessary. In the note Willett demonstrated how concerned he was about his appearance. He asked for a new suit, a beaver hat, a pair of green glasses, a new pair of boots, black cosmetics to color his hair and a 32-caliber revolver to defend himself. The pocket rifle was also 32-caliber.

Retrial

Initially Justice Landon ordered a retrial. His decision was based on the judge's allowing the admission of testimony of people who been involved with Willett during the period between the early arrest and the time he was originally charged. He had been denied an attorney and his rights had, therefore, been denied.

The retrial was not held as planned in January of 1882. Instead the battle over a retrial was taken through the entire appeal structure of the state. Willett's case languished in the judicial system while he sat helplessly in the county jail. Finally, in March of 1883, a retrial was ordered. The next available session was in September of 1883 so Willett would spend more than two and a half years waiting in the jail to learn his fate.

In May of 1883, Charles Hughes' friend and public servant General Barrett of Washington County died. Because Barrett and Hughes were friends and both agnostic Barrett had asked that Hughes make the final comments at his wake. Barrett's obituary offers some real insights into Hughes. Both men had a contingent of friends based on their ability to make others feel comfortable in there presence while they told stories or argued some point of law or politics. The homes of both men were open to men interested in debate and the stories of man. *The Troy Times* had these remarks about Hughes:

> ...a genial, whole souled, generous hearted, story telling, fun loving mortal whose soul is attuned by all the chords of sympathy and love to the music of the heavenly spheres when sung by the immortals. They (his friends) that in his great heart he harbors malice toward none; but with a charity as all pervading as the atmosphere he breathes spreads the mantle of his forgiveness over the misdeeds of mankind, and holds his humanity so universal that it includes in his ample scope the entire brotherhood of the human race. Wherever he goes sunshine follows in his footsteps, and smiles dissolve the tears and scowls of a frowning world.

What is most interesting is that many people went to General Barrett's wake just to hear Hughes explain his views on death. They were disappointed when a court date kept the master of discourse from attending.

The forgiveness credited to Hughes, if true, is the true measure of this man. He and his wife had had four children. By the time of the Willett trial all four of their children had died. None made it to be adults. Perhaps it was the knowledge of the meaning of life that drove Hughes so hard to defend people whose lives were to be taken from them.

***

Throughout the three years of waiting for a

trial, Willett was continuously incarcerated in a jail in Lake George. On occasion newspapers carried reports about how people who, while visiting the resort, would stop at his cell window and talk to him. According to those who met George Willett he had lost his color and was now pale from his long incarceration, which had kept him away from the sun. To the many people who met Willett in this fashion he was amiable and more importantly seemed incapable of the crime for which he had been convicted. Willett was allowed the freedom of walking the corridors of the jail during the day. He was also allowed unlimited visitors. He seemed to relish the attention and became somewhat a site to visit while on holiday in what is now Lake George.

To occupy his time Willett took up whittling for a hobby. First he carved a set of interlocking wooden chain links. Later he broke up his cigar boxes to make little wooden planks, which he later assembled into a miniature church. There were always people trying to make money off any situation. Willett was able to get an agent who took the small church around and charged people to see Willett's work. The agent was able to raise enough money so that Willett was able to buy a new suit for his second trial.

In sharp contrast to Willett's entrepreneurial endeavors, a question was also coming out concerning the expense that the county had incurred at Willett's trial. It was reported that Willett had cost the county in excess of $10,000, an appreciable sum in these times. Comparisons were made to a trial of the same length in Bennington Vermont, which took as long and only cost $5,000. What made the cost even less tenable to the county's taxpayers was the fact that Willett was not a resident and Pair had only lived in the county for eight months. Suddenly, pockets of people wanted Willett to be an issue in the past tense. Whether he was released or hanged was of little consequence; what mattered was that he no longer cost the taxpayers money.

For the people a second problem started to develop. District Attorney Howard was only narrowly victorious in the election of 1882. Some

WILLETT'S SECOND TRIAL IN PROGRESS
PICTURE IS CREDITED TO STODDARD
TAKING PICTURES IN COURT WAS NOT ALLOWED
THE PHOTOGRAPHER SUPPOSEDLY SLIPPED CAMERA INTO THE ROOM UNDER A BLANKET
PICTURE COURTESY OF LAKE GEORGE HISTORICAL ASSOCIATION

newspapers held that if it had not been for the creation of the Greenback Party, which split the Republican vote, Howard never would have been reelected. So deep was some of the animosity toward Howard that *The Glens Falls Republican*, a weekly newspaper wrote a series of disparaging commentaries on Howard and his lack of professionalism. They commented on how they were upset to watch as he stormed out of a supervisors meeting when they criticized the expenses he had approved relating to the Willett trial. *The Republican* also compared the skill style and competence of Howard to that of Hughes. Politically, the period between trials was a very uncomfortable time for Howard. A local newspaper waging war at the most personal level is an attack that few of us could ever withstand.

When the second trial of Willett was commencing in late September of 1883, the local interest was every bit as intense as it had been for the first trial. There were some major differences between the two trials. The first difference probably did not favor either side. It had been decided that the second trial would be before Judge Landon of Schenectady. Landon, although still relatively young, was a true jurist and was noted for his handling of difficult trials and the questions of evidence that they presented. The next difference was a blow to the prosecution. During the intervening two years between the trials the letters that had been in Willett's trunk had all disappeared. These were the handwritten proof that an intimate relationship between Jennie Pair and Willett existed. The final major difference favored the defense. A few weeks before the trial, and no on could say exactly when, Alvina Terrault disappeared. When asked on the stand for her whereabouts neither her husband, father or anyone else could say where she was nor were they absolutely sure when she had disappeared. The other major difference was the introduction of new witnesses. And finally, Jennie Pair did not attend this trial. Though her absence was a minor point it did cause the public to lose interest.

The prosecution put three new witnesses on the stand each of whom said that they had seen Willett in Glens Falls the evening of the murder. Hughes had a great time at these new witnesses' expense. Under direct examination they would say where and under what conditions they had seen Willett. When Howard finished his direct examination of the first witness or two he must have sat down, glowing in the assurance that their testimony would resolve the case and reestablish his reputation. Then the ever-clever Hughes would take over the examination. Hughes knew that when it came to taking the integrity away from a witness the devil was in the detail. Hughes would gently pick away at the person's memory. He would eat away at their credibility, demonstrating for the jury how these people suddenly had a perfect recollection of seeing a stranger, Willett, yet could not remember relatively simple things that they had done on the same day. If detail didn't get the new witness he would ask why they had not testified in the first case. There was no logic he couldn't oppose. His skill at attacking a witness was amazing, since he did it in a gentle, non-threatening way.

One witness had actually seen Willett in jail when the witness had visited Caldwell. Although there was a debate as to whether the intent was a visit (the defense's position) or an inadvertent casual glance (the witness' description of the event), it was only after this visit that the man could identify Willett. The fact that the way the district attorney learned of the man claiming to see Willett was based on a conversation that Howard had with the man while the man was doing some carpentry at Howard's house added little to his credibility.

The only way a witness faced with the probability of being questioned by Hughes ever left the stand feeling good was when Hughes said "no questions of this witness."

One other principle witness was not allowed to testify the same way as he had in the first trial. The man in question was a customer of Willett's and was shaved regularly by him. This man was not allowed to say he saw Willett walking on the railroad tracks toward Glens Falls on the night of the murder. The man was only allowed to say he saw a man who resembled Willett. The reasoning for the change was that the man had not made an immediate identification, but rather had made the connection after he realized that Willett was a suspect in the case.

Howard knew the importance of the letters if he were to demonstrate a motive. It was imperative for a guilty verdict that they get introduced into evidence. With the letters missing Howard asked the judge to have them read from the transcripts of the first trial. Justice Landon heard his motion then listened to Hughes' objection. On a technicality the judge only allowed the first letter into evidence. This was the letter whose contents were so disgusting that they never appeared in the newspaper. The other letters, including the one from Pair, were not admitted.

Clearly, the prosecution's case was much weaker this time than at the first trial. Without the letters they had trouble demonstrating a motive. The new witnesses brought in to identify Willett had not accomplished their objective. Adding to these losses was the inability of one of the other witness to make a positive identification of Willett on the railroad tracks. The only witness that would say positively that he had seen Willett on the streets of Glens Falls that night was Officer Bitley. The problem with Bitley was he stood to gain a portion of the one thousand-dollar reward if Willett was convicted.

There were four new witnesses for the defense. Two were brought in to defend the character of the man who owned the diner in Albany. This is the diner where Willett claimed to have spent the evening of the murder, eating his dinner. These character witnesses were brought in based on the attack that had been made on the owner in the first trial. Since these two were only there to support his reputation their late addition was more logical and acceptable. They explained for the jury that the man only rented the storefront and was therefore not responsible for the hole in the wall that led to the den of iniquity. Learning from Hughes, the master of undermining a witness, the prosecutors sought to discredit these witnesses. To some degree they were successful when

the witnesses refused to answer the question why they were asked to leave the Albany police force. The third new witness was Willett's aged father. He was brought into the trial to talk of his son's difficult upbringing, "not hav'n a ma, and such like that," His father admitted "hav'n a litt'l trouble with his memory" when he couldn't "member when he'd seen his daughter [Adeline] last." The fourth witness was a different gunsmith.

In this second trail the defense used John Nelson, a gunsmith from Troy. Nelson had proved himself a competent defense witness in the Billings trial. The difference between the two trials was that the gun the prosecution claimed was used in the Billings trial was clearly not the weapon that had killed the wife. In contrast the gun used on Pair was in all probability the actual weapon, so Nelson was not as successful.

One thing was certain, Judge Landon had run such a legally proper trial no further appeal would be sustained. To the observers in the courtroom the fact that this would be his last chance became more apparent on Willett's face as the trial progressed. The word among those who had followed the case closely was that the most Willett could hope for was that the jury would be unable to reach agreement.

Even having two years to prepare, the defense was not much stronger at this trial than in the first trial. It was obvious to the numerous observers that had attended the trial that the outcome of the case rested solely in how much weaker the prosecution's presentation was.

Judge Landon's charge to the jury lasted a little less than an hour. He talked of how the defense had never raised the issue of Pair's death being a suicide so therefore it had to be a murder. The question for the jury was, had the prosecution proved beyond a reasonable doubt that the gun used was the pocket rifle, and if so had Willett pulled the trigger?

The jury only deliberated for three hours. When the courthouse bell rang later that night the majority of people in Caldwell tried to get into the courthouse. The space was totally inadequate to hold the throng that had gathered to hear the verdict read. Those that were able to get inside watched as Willett was brought into the room. He was noticeably paler and had lost the arrogance that he had become known for.

Despite the crowded conditions those in the room stood in absolute silence as Judge Landon asked if they had reached a verdict. The foreman responded that they had agreed. Landon asked for their verdict and the foreman responded, "Not guilty."

When the verdict was read, a roar rang up from Willett's supporters. The traditional smile that people had become accustomed to had reappeared on Willet's face. He was immediately released from the court. He led the group of supporters as they went to the rail station where he and his father caught the next train north. By late that night they were back in Burlington, Vermont.

When the verdict was read, those close to the sixty-year-old Hughes heard him say as he slumped back into his seat, "No more murder trials. I have had enough."

Willett had left in such a hurry his pocket rifle could not be returned to him. Logically the bailiff gave the pocket rifle to a man of peace, Hughes.

The next day there were rumors that Jennie Pair and George Willett had been married. The newspapers checked with several family members and were assured that no marriage had taken place.

***

After the trial the community wondered why they had spent close to $20,000 on the trial of a man that was not even convicted. The immediate reaction was that the jury had failed in its responsibility.

The criticism was so great that the foreman of the jury wrote a letter to the newspaper, explaining what had happened. He noted that as soon as they were alone they took a straw poll. At that time the jury stood nine to three for acquittal. They reviewed the evidence regarding some of the concerns that jurors mentioned then took a second vote. At this point they stood eleven to one for acquittal. Immediately the one other juror

switched his vote and they stood unanimous for acquittal.

The disapproval with the verdict was probably misguided. The letters had been absolutely essential to the prosecution. Whoever had taken them for a souvenir had changed the course of history and added to Willett's life.

Visiting the Scene Today

Fort Edward has not changed much since the days when Pair and Willett would walk from the Pair house on North Canal Street to the barbershop on Broadway. The barbershop is now the little diner at 134 Broadway. You can go have a reasonably priced meal in the same spot that Willett and Pair worked side by side. This was of course in the days before Jennie "turned George Willett's head."

The barbershop where the murder happened was taken down a few years later. It was replaced by a three-story structure on the east side of Glen Street. It is always amazing that the stories that are uncovered are so totally forgotten. People who work and live within feet of these atrocities don't even know what happened. The building recently underwent reconstruction. One has to wonder if the new owner has any idea of what occurred on the site of venture.

The village of Caldwell was renamed the Village of Lake George. It can be reasonably assumed that virtually all the tourists that walk by the old courthouse on the main street are unaware that it was the site of a pair of trials that almost bankrupted the county. Here was the home of a murderer who was released as much for lack of evidence as for an equally important reason, the simple fact that the taxpayers were tired of paying for his exorbitantly expensive trials.

The former courthouse has been converted into a museum. A visitor can actually walk in jail area where Willett spent three years of his life. The church that he constructed to pay for a new suit is on display in the main gallery. The courtroom where the trial occurred is intact and one can actual sit where Willett, Hill and Hughes sat

THE SCENE OF THE MURDER
A FEW YEARS AFTER THE CRIME THE BARBER SHOP
WAS TORN DOWN AND REPLACED BY
THIS STOREFRONT

during the trial.

The great defense lawyer and defender of the legal rights of the poor, Charles Hughes, lived until April of 1887. Whether in addition to his legal skills, he was a profit and as he said at the end never undertook another murder trail is yet to be discovered. His home has been consumed by entropy but a trip to Union Cemetery between Hudson Falls and Fort Edward will take you to his family's final resting place.

The cemetery where John Pair and his wife are buried was never mentioned in the records. What we do know is that it was in Hudson Falls. That would imply it was either the Union Cemetery or the Catholic Cemetery behind it. However, Union Cemetery has been fully indexed and the Pair name does not appear. The Catholic Cemetery was not even in existence until years

later. Since the funeral party went to Clark's Hotel to warm up after the interment, it is logical that the cemetery was on the south side of Hudson Falls. This could have been a real dilemma except for the memory of a local policeman. There is an old cemetery, named Baker Cemetery just off John Street in Hudson Falls. It is nestled behind the homes and only accessible through a small gate between two houses. In this cemetery there are numerous graves of people who could not afford quality stones and the names have disappeared forever. It is in this simple cemetery that the Pairs most assuredly rest. A visit is worth the adventure.

The Old Established
Butterfield Livery Stable.

[ESTABLISHED 1827.]

No. 12 Main Street, Utica, N. Y.

This favorite establishment is the oldest and most complete in everything that makes up a Livery Stable that can be found in the world, and is always ready to furnish the public with

Horses and Carriages

Of first-class style and with faithful Drivers, for Parties, Weddings, &c. &c.

AT PRICES TO SUIT THE TIMES.

Funerals Attended with Carriages and an elegant hearse if desired.

We only ask our share of Patronage, and having been in the business OVER THIRTY YEARS, we think we know the wants of the public.

☞ REMEMBER 12 MAIN STREET,

THEO. F. BUTTERFIELD,

Proprietor.

Major Sources

Newspapers

Albany Argus
Albany Morning ExpressThe Ballston Spa Journal
The Batavia Daily News
The Batavia Times
The Daily Saratogian
The Glens Falls Messenger
The Glens Falls Republican
The National Police Gazette
The New York Times
The Saratoga Sentinel
The Troy Daily Times
The Troy Press
The Utica Observer
The Utica Weekly

Museums & Libraries

The Crandall Library (Glens Falls)
The Holland Patton Museum
The Lake George Historical Society
The New York State Library
The Richmond Memorial Library
The Saratoga County Historian
The Saratoga Public Library
The Utica Public Library
The Warren County Archives
The Washington County Archives

Coming August 2003